DANCING
WITH THE
SACRED

KARL E. PETERS

DANCING
WITH THE
SACRED

Evolution, Ecology, and God

TRINITY PRESS INTERNATIONAL
Harrisburg, Pennsylvania

Trinity Press International, P.O. Box 1321, Harrisburg, PA 17105
Trinity Press International is a division of The Morehouse Group.

Cover design: Laurie Westhafer

Library of Congress Cataloging-in-Publication Data

Peters, Karl Edward, 1939–
    Dancing with the sacred : evolution, ecology, and God / Karl E. Peters.
        p.   cm.
    Includes bibliographical references and index.
    ISBN 1-56338-393-4 (pbk. : alk. paper)
    1. Philosophical theology. 2. Evolution – Religious aspects – Christianity.
    3. Human ecology – Religious aspects – Christianity.   I. Title.
BT55 .P48 2002
210 – dc21

2002000556

Printed in the United States of America

02   03   04   05   06   07   10   9   8   7   6   5   4   3   2   1

Contents

Preface

During my career as a teacher of philosophy and religious studies and a scholar in religion and science, I have been developing a way of understanding the presence of God in my life that is compatible with the ideas of modern science. This not because I think science has all the answers but because the traditional understanding of God that I grew up with did not help me experience the presence of the sacred in my own life. Traditional approaches offer much insight into the sacred, but by themselves they have not provided a practical theology that has been sufficient for my own living.

Seeking a practical theology has led me to engage in a thought experiment. I have come to think of God as the creative process or creative event rather than a being who creates the world. Essentially, this new way of thinking regards everything as events or processes rather than as beings or substances. It is not so much a shift in religious thinking as in philosophical thinking regarding the general categories we use to conceptualize all existence. It is called process thinking.

Many religious thinkers today are process theologians. Most of them use personal metaphors and models in portraying God. My own approach has been to explore nonpersonal metaphors and models. Others who have used this approach call what I'm doing "naturalistic theism." As a naturalistic theist I do not deny that God is more than the world, but I do want to focus continually on how we can know and be related to God in our natural world. This to me is crucial for religious living.

The nonpersonal model of God I will describe in this book is based on the Darwinian idea of random variation and natural selection. Suggesting that God is a process with two aspects, I philosophically generalize this model to all levels of existence — cosmic evolution, biological evolution, cultural evolution, and developments in our own lives. One aspect of this two-part process is the emergence of new possibilities in nature, human history, and personal living. The other is the selection of some of these possibilities to continue. With this model I suggest that God — conceived of as the creative process — is like a dance. By participating in the creative process we are dancing with the sacred.

Dancing with the sacred, or living daily with the living God, is important for me in finding meaning and purpose in life. It also is important for living harmoniously with the rest of life on our ever-changing planet. As a result of the rise of Western democracies, free-market economies, and modern science and technology in the last few centuries, many of us have come to enjoy increased material prosperity. At the same time we are beginning to recognize that our modern life-style is harming other creatures, diminishing the functioning of ecosystems, and altering our global climate patterns. We worry that what we are doing to our planet will adversely affect the lives of our children and grandchildren. So the question arises: how can we relate to the sacred creative process in ways that will motivate us to live for the good of our entire planet and not just for ourselves?

While I think of God as a sacred dance that continuously gives rise to new possibilities for existence and selects some of those to continue, I realize that loss and suffering are also a result of this process. People get sick and die. Species evolve to extinction. Occasionally natural catastrophes alter the functioning of planet Earth, bringing about mass extinctions. What might it mean to live with hope and to work toward the greater well-being of ourselves and the planet in the midst of suffering, loss, and perishing?

This book is an exploration of these issues. I use some ideas from modern science, the world's religions, and my own experience with family and friends to suggest how it is possible to be religious in evolutionary terms. First, I try to see how the sacred can be understood as the creative activity of nature, human history, and individual life. Second, I explore how we might understand ourselves in a way that motivates us to live more in harmony with the rest of life on planet Earth. Third, I try to see how we might live meaningfully in a world in which suffering and death are creatively intertwined with life.

This is a thought experiment. Many people experience the sacred in their lives from the perspective of traditional personal understandings of God. Many are addressing environmental issues inspired by their own religious traditions. And many use traditional ways of understanding the sacred and our world in coping with the tragedies of existence in their lives and on our planet. I appreciate all these resources for living. As a teacher in courses on the world's religions, science and religion, and environmental ethics, I have explored many traditional ways of thinking with my students. I find much wisdom in religious traditions.

However, I also find that my mind has been shaped by the world view of modern science. I live with a scientific understanding of things in my daily life, and I use the fruits of the natural and social sciences to clean my house, gain knowledge of what is happening in other parts of the world, treat my illnesses, understand the workings of my brain, and find insight into my personal relationships with others. For me it is only one more step to ask how scientific knowledge might help me in my religious living. Some of what I've learned I share with you in this book — as an experiment in a new way of thinking about God and the meaning of life.

I have come to understand the writing of this book as an instance of my participating in the sacred creative process. The ideas of many people — known and unknown — have interacted to shape my thinking. I am grateful for the thinking of ancient religious people as well as the thinking of contemporary scientists, philosophers, and theologians. Their work has continually transformed my own thinking in ways that have increased my understanding, made my living more meaningful, and provided personal guidance.

In particular I am grateful for those who have listened to my ideas and responded to them honestly and helpfully. Many of the ideas were initially presented to Unitarian Universalist societies throughout central Florida. Others grew out of courses I have taught on religion and science at Rollins College, as a result of discussions with questioning undergraduate students. The general tone of the book was shaped by the caring interactions among the members of the Spiritual Autobiography Group of the Unitarian Society of Hartford, Connecticut.

An earlier version of the first half of the book was discussed in an adult class of people from different denominations; the class was sponsored by the Unitarian Society of Hartford. Members of the Institute on Religion in an Age of Science gave me useful suggestions on the entire manuscript at the IRAS annual conference in 1999. Further feedback came from members of a book discussion group in Central Florida sponsored by Mensa, Free Thinkers, and Unitarian Universalists. In particular I appreciate the helpful and encouraging comments of Elizabeth Bjorkman, Michael Cavanaugh, Willem Drees, Thomas Gilbert, Ursula Goodenough, Philip Hefner, Steve Helle, Ernst Mayr, Michael Ruse, and Roy Starling. More recently George Brooks, Eric Chaisson, Gordon Kaufman, Edward Kolsby, Holmes Rolston III, and Marilyn Stewart have provided useful criticism. The encouragement and critique from these group discussions and individuals have led me to rewrite and revise parts of an earlier manuscript into this book. I give special thanks to Henry Carrigan and the publishing team at Trinity Press International. They have provided enthusiastic support and expert editing. Because of their efforts and those of others mentioned above, the book is a better creation. The problems that still remain are due to the limits of my own mind to digest and express all that might improve it further.

I have been blessed by the people in my life, especially those with whom I have lived. My father, Norman J. Peters, provided me with a model for how to live with a faith that is open to new futures and a realism that knows when to let go. My biological mother, Lethel Wolter Peters, nurtured me even in the midst of her lengthy terminal illness. My second mother, Alice Krautsch Peters, has shown me what it is like to live according to the motto: "In whatever state I am, I have learned to be content." My uncle Arthur Peters, crippled for the sixty-six years of his life, showed me the importance of always welcoming people. My first wife, Carol Dzemske Peters, through her honest and courageous living and dying, helped me realize that my years of experimenting with the ideas of naturalistic theism paid off in helping me respond to the challenges of the last months of her life. My present wife, Marjorie Hall Davis, is a keen, like-minded intellect and a caring partner, with whom I am sharing the joys of new family and a hopeful future. She has provided valuable editorial assistance in making this book more readable.

These and many others have interacted with me in thoughtful and caring ways. They have helped me experience the presence of the sacred in my life.

✑ Chapter 1 ✑

Thinking about God in a New Way

The old rabbi came up to the podium after the lecture. In a quiet voice he said, "Thank you! Now I can believe in God again." I felt a kindred spirit. Even though we came from two different religions, Judaism and Christianity, we were both living and thinking within the world view of modern science. The world view of modern science is naturalistic. The focus of science is on the world of space-time that can be known through observation and through ideas that help us understand what is observed. For the rabbi and me this space-time world was also the focus of religious living. It was the place where meaning and purpose, where ultimate value, could be found. We were looking for a naturalistic God, the sacred that was embedded in the world.

We also were seeking a God that was compatible with evolutionary theory. The usual debates between creationists and evolutionists, while important for some people, did not help us know how to be religious in a scientific age. Neither did views suggesting that the God of Western religion created the world through the processes of evolution. Although such views are held even by some scientists, we were looking for a more integrated understanding of God and evolutionary theory, of God working creatively in the world and of Darwin's theory of random variation and natural selection.

This was the view of God that I had just presented in a lecture at a conference on religion and science. In my lecture I had suggested that God be imagined not as a being who creates the world but as the process of creation itself. I then went on to suggest that

1

the process of creation could be partly understood as a two-phase process, characterized as random variation and natural selection. Darwinian evolutionary theory could then be a way of understanding God, and the idea of God could be a way of seeing the value of continuing creation. It was my presentation of a Darwinian God to which the rabbi responded, "Thank you! Now I can believe in God again."

I had begun to think of God as the creative process when the way I had been taught to think about God no longer seemed credible to me. I grew up in a liberal Christian home, was a youth leader in my local church, had a religious experience that called me to the Christian ministry, was a fundamentalist, evangelical Christian in college, was first in my class at seminary, studied ecumenical theology in Germany, and enrolled in the Ph.D. program at Columbia University and Union Theological Seminary in New York City. By my second year in graduate school, I discovered I was an atheist.

My problem was that, while growing up in a Christian environment, I also had been educated in a scientific approach to life and the world. I was the son of an engineer, was educated in the public school system of Wisconsin, and my undergraduate philosophy professor was an empiricist (although I did not know it at the time). As I was soon to discover, I was a pragmatist, a practical thinker for whom "seeing is believing."

I could not experience God at work in the world. All the intellectual manipulating of Christian religious ideas simply broke down for me, because I could not attach them to my sense experiences. Furthermore, I had learned in seminary that God was a God of history, active in the world. If God was supposed to be present everywhere, shouldn't I and everyone else be able to experience God in everyday life? When I asked about this, I was told that we could experience the effects of God but not God. However, an alternative interpretation of events is also possible. All that happens could just as well be due to the workings of nature and human society. Why bring in God as an effective cause of world events, of events in my own life? I could see no reason to believe that God influences what happens in the world, unless one could somehow experience God. For me, I had to "see" to believe.

Being an atheist while getting my doctoral degree in religion felt very awkward. I felt the tension between my inherited faith and my developing naturalistic view of the world. However, two things came together to begin reshaping my thinking. One was an essay by Charles Sanders Peirce, the founder of American pragmatic philosophy. In "How to Make Our Ideas Clear," he said that we should define ideas, even abstract ideas, by the experiences we could expect to have if such an idea were credible.[1] Up to then I had defined the word "God" as a supreme, personal being. Such a God I could not observe. Who can observe a supreme, personal being? Could I, following Peirce, define the word "God" in terms of experiences? What kind of experiences?

During this time my wife and I had befriended a young woman with many problems. She came from a broken home, had a mother who had many men, was almost homeless, and was a devout Roman Catholic. Because I had graduated from seminary, I fancied I could counsel her. We met once a week and she talked about her problems. I don't think I helped her very much but she, without knowing it, helped me considerably. In spite of all the problems in her broken life, she would occasionally say, "Grace happened to me today." What a peculiar expression, "Grace happened to me today!" She was describing events, and when I listened to the kinds of events she described, I concluded they were events in which something good happened to her, beyond her control.

I took her idea of grace and, using the ideas of Peirce, wrote a paper titled "Pragmatism, Definitions, and God." In it I defined the word "God" as the "grace-type event." I described this kind of event as occurring when things beyond our control come together in such a way that they bring about good. After reading the paper, my professor and later my dissertation advisor, Daniel Day Williams, asked, "Have you ever read Henry Nelson Wieman?" "No," I said. Williams replied, "You should, you sound just like him." Wieman had been Williams's teacher at the University of Chicago. When I finally got around to reading his works, I discovered a person who had thought what I was trying to think twenty-five years earlier.[2]

Wieman wrote of God as the creative event, the creative process, the process of creative transformation. His God consisted of those interactions taking place among humans and between humans and the rest of the world that gave rise to truth, beauty, love, and community. The important thing for me was that I could observe such interactions. By defining God as an event or process, I could see God working in the world. I could again believe in God.

In my Ph.D. dissertation I showed how one could develop and test ideas about God by defining God as the creative process. I even argued that one could test ideas about God scientifically using experimental methods from social psychology. My dissertation explored how one could develop a "scientific theology."[3]

After completing my dissertation I began to enhance the work I was doing on Wieman by relating it to the thinking of Ralph Wendell Burhoe, the founding editor of *Zygon: Journal of Religion and Science.*[4] Wieman thought of God primarily as a social process, the process of creativity or creative interchange among humans. Only secondarily did Wieman consider this process in the natural world. Burhoe, however, helped me expand Wieman's concept into the creative system of evolving life in an evolving universe, which for me was a universal sacred activity present throughout the world.

With the idea of God as the universal creative process, continuously at work to give rise to new forms of existence — physical existence, life, and human community — I gained a deeper appreciation of how we are rooted in the cosmos. Evolutionary theory not only gave me a way to think about God as an activity continuously creating the universe. It also helped me to realize that we who live today are continuous with historical humans and their societies, including their religions. We are continuous with other forms of life. We are continuous with the energy that was present at the origins of the universe. This energy has undergone countless transformations into elemental forms of matter, stars, more complex atoms and molecules, life, humanity, and human society. We are the products of these transformations. As Robert Weston puts it poetically, we have come "Out of the Stars" — the result of the ongoing creativity that is the heart of the universe.

Out of the stars in their flight, out of the dust of eternity,
here have we come,
Stardust and sunlight, mingling through time and through
space.
Out of the stars have we come, up from time;
Time out of time before time in the vastness of space, earth
spun to orbit the sun,
Earth with the thunder of mountains newborn, the boiling of
seas.
Earth warmed by the sun, lit by sunlight:
This is our home; out of the stars have we come.
Mystery hidden in mystery, back through all time;
Mystery rising from rocks in the storm and the sea.
Out of the stars, rising from rocks and the sea, kindled by
sunlight on earth arose life.
Ponder this thing in your heart; ponder with awe:
Out of the sea to the land, out of the shallows came ferns.
Out of the sea to the land, up from darkness to light,
Rising to walk and to fly, out of the sea trembled life.
Ponder this thing in your heart, life up from sea;
Eyes to behold, throats to sing, mates to love.
Life from the sea, warmed by sun, washed by rain,
Life from within, giving birth, rose to love.
This is the wonder of time; this is the marvel of space;
Out of the stars swung the earth; life upon earth rose to love.
This is the marvel of life, rising to see and to know;
Out of your heart, cry wonder: sing that we live.[5]

The realization that we humans have emerged out of this long evolutionary process calls us to live responsibly. It calls us to respect and cherish all human beings, all life forms, our planet, and the entire universe as the results of a sacred creative process. More important, it calls us into communion with that process, to participate in it in realizing new good for humans in harmony with other life forms on our own planet. Living in communion with the sacred and cherishing all that it has created is a way of being religious in a scientific age.

Exploring what it means to be religious in the context of a scientific world view — using insights from Darwinian evolutionary theory and from an ecological understanding that we are all part of an interdependent web of existence woven by a sacred creative process — is what I want to share with you. In the next chapter I will describe more fully how science views the world and how it has helped to create a more unified life on Earth, the emerging global village. In chapter three I will discuss how we have evolved in such a way as to place our global village in peril and raise the question of how we can find human fulfillment in a way that also is in harmony with the workings of our planet. Then, in chapters four through eight I will offer a series of sketches of my present understanding of God or the Sacred, bringing together some ideas from ancient religious traditions and from modern science. In chapters nine through thirteen I will explore what it means to be a human being in an evolving universe, living in harmony with an evolving planet. In chapters fourteen through sixteen I will struggle with the problem of loss and suffering, sharing some of my own experience. Finally, in the last two chapters I will try to suggest what it means to be at home in our vast universe and on an ever changing planet, when all our efforts to preserve our earthly home might come to nothing because of cosmic events beyond our control. Through all this I hope it will become clear that those who accept a naturalistic view of the world based on modern science can find a way to live meaningfully and morally — to dance with the sacred.

✨ Chapter 2 ✨

Science and Societies in the Emerging Global Village

In my thinking, living, and teaching, I have come to hold three guiding concerns that lie at the heart of this book. First, what does it mean to try to understand myself and my world with knowledge from the contemporary sciences? Second, how can I begin to think and live in a culturally pluralistic world in a way that makes positive use of the variety of ways other people think and live? Third, how can I find the will to respond to the growing awareness that the way I and others are thinking and living is increasingly degrading the rest of our natural world, thereby putting our planet and ourselves in peril? This chapter will outline my first two concerns; the next chapter will focus on the third.

The term "global village" is often used to describe a phenomenon of which many are becoming more conscious. Recently I purchased a new German car, an American brand television set made in Taiwan, and an Italian-named microwave built in Korea. Coca Cola now sells in the People's Republic of China, and McDonalds sells hamburgers in Russia with beef from Brazil. The transportation and communication technologies of the last half of the twentieth century are making physical and mental travel more common. An airline flying from Chicago to San Francisco has an emergency instruction book printed in seven languages. We can circle the globe on the World Wide Web while staying at home. In so many ways we are economically and consciously becoming a global village.

The phrase global village conveys the idea that we are so interconnected with each other that it is as if we are living in a village. In villages people know everybody's business. While we don't literally know everybody's business in our world, we know more than ever before about the lives of other people as they are filtered through the media. Political reforms and revolutions, famines, international sports events, ecological disasters, explorations in space, swings in the stock market, peace initiatives, military build-ups — events that signify both the best and worst for humanity and the earth are shared daily via the media on a planet-wide basis. The amazing thing is not that everybody's business is coming home to us via scientific technology. The amazing thing is that we take it for granted, yet miss its significance.

Never before in the history of the world have so many known about so much. Never before have so many people with so many different belief systems, values, and styles of life become aware of one another. In the courses I teach on religion and science, I try to help my students appreciate how they are among the first generations in the history of humanity to develop the awareness of the many different ways people have lived. We are living during the dawn of a new era; in all the five billion years that our planet has spun and circled our Sun, we are now spinning each new day closer and closer to the new age of planet-encircling interdependence.

The new age that is dawning is an age of increasing scientific unity. When we buy our cars and television sets, when we see the TV satellite pictures of weather formations covering half our globe, when we communicate by using cellular phones, fax machines, e-mail, and the World Wide Web, we experience firsthand how the scientific technology developed mostly since the middle of the twentieth century is unifying the world. Scientific unity means, first, that contemporary scientific technology is the vehicle bringing the people on Earth closer and closer together.

As this happens scientific unity acquires a second meaning. With the increased use of scientific technology people come more and more to rely on the assumptions and methods that make such technology possible. People come to rely less on the authority of their elders and ancestors. Instead, they learn to test the new technology to see how it works, to see whether it accomplishes the promised results, to see whether it makes their lives better, or at least easier.

As people become educated in the scientific disciplines, they learn that the experimental method is the way to find out if a machine or an idea — or an idea translated into a machine — works. An idea is accepted not because some political or religious leader says it is true. It is accepted not because some ancient sacred text says it is true. An idea is accepted because it can be translated into expected observations of what will happen. If what is predicted actually occurs, the idea is supported; if not, the idea needs to be changed or rejected. Along with the increasing technical nature of the world-wide village, the empirical method is becoming part of the thinking of more and more human beings.

A third meaning of scientific unity involves the way in which people are coming to view the world. Let's imagine that we are scientists. As scientists we do not use personal metaphors and models to understand what happens. We do not attempt to explain how things happen by appealing to hidden personal realities that think, intend actions, and then perform actions. For example, when we trip over a branch that has fallen in our path, we do not see this as caused by an invisible, malevolent, personal spirit as some of our ancestors did. As scientists, neither do we see all events as caused by an unseen personal deity, existing beyond the universe yet acting on the universe. Instead, as we assume a scientific view of things — which is more and more common as people use the technology and experimental methods of science — we see the causes of things in nonpersonal terms, in terms of laws and forces. A shorthand way of saying this is that we understand the causes of what happens naturalistically. The world view of modern science is experimental naturalism. Naturalism means that everything is energy-matter and the information according to which energy-matter is organized. It also means that the causes of things are not personal, mental, and intentional — except when personal creatures such as humans and probably some animals are involved.

To summarize, in helping create a global village, science is unifying the world in three ways: through the use of scientific technology, through the use of empirical methods, and through seeing the causes of natural events in nonpersonal rather than in mental or personal terms. The new age that has been dawning with each new day of the spinning earth for the past century or so — the new age of increasing worldwide interconnectedness — is a scientific age.

However, as we become more unified through science and its technology, we also become more conscious of all that divides us, of the different cultural systems, of the different religious traditions that make up the complex heritage of humanity. How can we, with our own particular traditions, come to understand and appreciate those who are culturally different?

Suppose we were to take time to study human history regarding how people thought about those who were beyond their own society. With few exceptions, such as laws of kindness to individual strangers, I expect we would find that the "others" were regarded as the out-group and even as enemies. Systems of morality that apply to those within a society do not apply to those outside, because the outsiders are seen as somehow less than fully human. Hence it is wrong to kill, rape, or steal from members of one's own society. But these acts are often permissible against members of other societies and even against those existing in our own society when they are thought of as property or less that fully human.

With this attitude toward the outsider, it has been common to want to convert other societies to our way of life, to evangelize them into our religion, to "humanize" them. Or we have thought it morally acceptable to enslave them, to put them on reservations, or even to exterminate them. This kind of thinking dominated the minds of many European settlers as they confronted the native inhabitants of the Americas. It still influences many people's attitudes towards other cultures. As long as they learn our language and acquire our customs and values, they are our friends. But if they represent other basic life-styles, they are regarded with suspicion, in the way one regards enemies. Of course, people from other societies often have the same attitude toward us; we are the ones who can't be trusted. While there may be legitimate, rational grounds for judging particular practices of any society negatively, all too often such negative judgments simply illustrate the prejudicial stance that many have taken regarding outsiders when they interact and possibly compete with one another.

In the past, prejudicial attitudes supported intersocietal conflicts that were relatively small in scale. The weapons of war inflicted harm mostly on those directly participating in battle. However, one of the terrible fruits of scientific technology is that weapons of war can be so widely devastating, inflicting death and damage not just to warriors but to civilians and to the earth itself. We don't even need to imagine nuclear war to realize this, although even a limited nuclear war with the threat of nuclear winter would provoke havoc over much of our planet. We need only to remember the effects of the chemical warfare in Vietnam — the napalm and Agent Orange — on humans, animals, and vegetation. If people continue to believe that they, their life-style, or their religion are better than those of others, if people continue to hold attitudes that regard those who are different as people to be converted, enslaved, or destroyed, the new dawning scientific age could well be the last age of civilized life on our planet for a long time to come. We must change our attitudes and find better ways to understand and appreciate our cultural and religious diversity.

In my own intellectual journey, I have come to think that a key to understanding cultural and religious diversity, so as to enhance the possibilities of peace in the emerging global village, is a general theory of evolution. This is the idea that, since the beginning of the universe about fourteen billion years ago, change, growth, and development are to be regarded as fundamental to the nature of things.[1] It is the idea that reality is continually creative — creative of galaxies, stars, planetary systems, life, and cultures. It is the idea that this creative reality promotes diversity. It is the idea that diversity can be used as a catalyst for further creation. As different atoms, organisms, and ideas interact with one another, that very interaction provides the possibility that new forms of existence, life, or social relationship will emerge.

With this new understanding of an evolving universe, I also have come to affirm a traditional understanding of its value. One way of expressing the value of all that continually is created is the phrase that is repeated in the first chapter of the Hebrew Bible: "And God saw that it was good."[2] This means that everything in the world has its own inherent worth. Therefore, one can marvel at and appreciate the rich diversity of life and the variety of social systems in which humans have been able to live. Appreciating diversity and variety does not mean one must value equally every form of life or every way of living. Evolving life and evolving societies are dynamic. Ways of living that once were effective may no longer be helpful. As times and situations change, what once was accepted as valuable and right may now be regarded as less valuable and even wrong. However, both my new understanding of the evolving universe and the affirmations of the Hebrew Bible suggest that diminishing life, hindering human flourishing, and obstructing the ongoing process of creation are wrong. The rich diversity in our world is to be prized as the result of eons of effort by that which continually creates the world as long as the diversity continues to enable the process of further creation.

The interactions brought about by contemporary science and its technology are a part of this ongoing creativity in the universe. These interactions are giving rise to something new on the face of the earth — a planet-wide interconnectedness that some call the global village. As this village continues to emerge, we should respect different social systems, even if we do not endorse everything they do, because all societies, including our own, are the result of past creative activity — of biological and cultural evolution on our planet creating an increasing richness of life forms and life-styles. We also should respect this richness of diversity, because it is a resource for further creativity. We can participate in further creation by allowing people with different patterns of thinking and acting — even thinking and acting religiously — to suggest new ways of thinking and acting for ourselves. When we combine these new ways with our old patterns of living and thinking, we will discover that we are being born anew. Our own living will be enriched because we come to understand more, are enabled to do more. Our world will be enriched because with ongoing creative transformation people will become more accepting and appreciative of differences in a pluralistic yet cooperating world system.

Isn't such continuing to be born again better than trying to convert or destroy one another? I think it is, for this reason. By trying to live creatively with differences, by trying to let the differences between us and others lead to recombinations of thought and practice, we are being consistent with what an evolving universe, an evolving planet, and an evolving humanity have been engaged in for fourteen billion years. In an evolving universe, I would rather be on the side of new creation than on the side of destruction.[3] In the emerging global village, I would rather heed the ancient commandment given by Yahweh, the creative reality in the universe as understood by the Hebrew people: "I have set before you life or death, blessings and curses. Choose life so that you and your descendants may live."[4] Whether the new dawning global village, the new dawning age of scientific unity in the midst of traditional cultural diversity, will be an age of death and darkness or an age of life and light, is a choice that is up to human beings in all societies around our world.

Peril in the Global Village

How we think influences how we act. How we think about ourselves in relation to the rest of the world in part determines how we behave toward ourselves, other humans, our planet, and its creatures. Many people today are thinking in ways that put our global village in peril, simply because they have not included the rest of our planet in their thinking about the global village. Until recently I limited my concept of the global village only to what is human — the emerging interweaving of the plurality of human cultures in a scientific age. Others do that too. However, the current scientific picture of our human origins shows that we have come out of the stars and that we are a significant part of the flourishing of life on our planet.

In his book *Cosmic Dawn*, Eric Chaisson sketches the fourteen-billion-year-history of the universe. He shows how we have emerged through a series of long and arduous processes of cosmic evolution.[1] A part of our origin is in what he calls the "first great event in the history of the universe" — the emergence of matter out of energy. After the "big bang's" initial expansion and cooling down, hydrogen and helium atoms were formed. Because of fluctuations and unequal densities, the energy and gas at the dawn of creation did not disperse uniformly but began to condense into galactic clouds. Within the galactic clouds uneven densities of hydrogen and helium coalesced further to form smaller gas clouds that would become stars. Under the forces of gravity and friction, hydrogen and helium clouds collapsed and heated up until they ignited, fusing their hydrogen into more helium and releasing tremendous amounts of energy. Stars were born. Matter, operating according to natural laws, began to control energy. This was the first great event, the first great transformation in the history of the universe.

Some of the stars had much more mass than our Sun and, following natural laws, burned up their fuel rather quickly. Then they went through a series of expansions and collapses, following natural laws, until some of the most massive stars collapsed and then rebounded in explosions called supernovae. Such explosions created temperatures high enough to fuse the heavier elements out of lighter ones. These elements, along with interstellar hydrogen and helium, formed new clouds that condensed again to form second generation stars, and in some instances planets. Our solar system and Earth were born this way, out of the "dust" resulting from exploding supernovae. Our planet, its life forms, and our own bodies contain the oxygen, nitrogen, carbon, iron, and other elements from earlier exploding stars. We are "star stuff" — a part of the matter that was created earlier in the universe's history.

We humans are a particular kind of matter called life, and we are a particular kind of life. We are scientific-technological life — what Chaisson calls the "second great event" in the history of the universe. With us, mind has begun to control matter and energy. We have a brain that has invented linguistic communication, mathematics, and tools. We have learned to use fire, invented the wheel, and developed irrigation systems and aqueducts. We have manufactured steel plows for turning hard soil, built internal combustion engines, created nuclear power plants, and rocketed into space. We have used the knowledge of living organisms and of chemistry to control disease, and now we are developing the capacity to engineer our own genetic self-replication. We have built schools to develop human minds, established multinational corporations, increased the material standard of living of a small percentage of human beings, and invented a telecommunications industry to inform more and more people about what is happening around the world. This second great event in the history of the universe has occurred for the most part within the last one hundred years in the fourteen-billion-year-history of the universe. In this second great event, scientific human culture has emerged. This culture is supported by the rest of nature — the larger global village of planet Earth as a whole. And we have placed the total global village, including ourselves, in peril.

It is not that we have been intentionally destructive, although some have knowingly damaged the environment and other humans. Disasters such as Three Mile Island and Love Canal may be examples of human moral evil. So might regional acid rain altering the flourishing of trees in the Smokey Mountains. However, we are learning that human technological activity, which is carried out for purposes we consider good, is contributing to global warming, the greenhouse effect, and major changes in climate. Learning about such unintended consequences now makes us morally responsible when we continue the practices contributing to the phenomena that place our planet in peril.

There are good reasons for much that we have done. We have simply been using our minds, our science, and resulting technology to improve our human chances for survival and well-being. For example, beginning with the discovery of bacteria by Louis Pasteur, we have used knowledge gained in biology to improve sanitation and control infectious diseases. This has led to a decline in the rate of infant mortality, which in turn has been one of the major causes of our human population explosion. Our rapidly growing population, combined with our quest for an ever higher material standard of living, is expanding the human habitat around our globe at the expense of the habitats of other species. One instance of this expansion, deforestation, has contributed to a dramatic increase in the rate of extinction of other species. These changes in turn are altering the functioning of ecosystems, perhaps to the point that we are damaging the infrastructure of our planet on which we humans also depend.

Likewise, increased knowledge in physics, applied in engineering, has developed the internal combustion engine that utilizes the rich reserves of oil converted to gasoline for cars. This has made us much more mobile, and in this sense more "free," than ever before in history. In the United States in particular, as Bill Moyers in his video interview of biochemist Jessica Tuchman Matthews points out, the myth of the open road is very powerful, so powerful that for many it is hard to conceive what life without automobiles would be like.[2] Automobiles continue to be one of the primary sources of carbon dioxide and other greenhouse gases that threaten to alter our global climate. Even though there already are alternative engines that emit less of such gases, the economics of business and the current political climate make it difficult to put new technologies into practice.

Then there is "better living through chemistry": pesticides and fungicides to improve food production, refrigerants to help preserve our food and to cool our homes and cars, fuels for transportation, paints to beautify our homes, synthetic fabrics to wear, detergents to keep our clothes and dishes clean, synthetic vitamins to keep us healthy, cosmetics to beautify our bodies, and mood controlling drugs to help us feel better. What power the human mind has over matter! And so much of the power is used to do what is thought to be good for human beings. Yet we are now beginning to see more clearly that this good is at the expense of the planet: a variety of toxic wastes and other pollutants endanger the health and lives of humans, animals, plants, and ecosystems alike.

Yet, with all these developments, we usually have not been intentionally and knowingly bad people. Furthermore, we know much of what we must do to mitigate the harmful effects that have resulted from our good intentions. We must control human population growth, develop more fuel efficient and less polluting technologies, replant forests, reduce our consumption of things that are not necessary, and shift toward economies that repair and reuse material goods instead of throwing them away and replacing them.

However, even though we know what we can do, we usually do not do it. A major hindrance to changing our perilous behavior is our lack of will. This is the problem of moral motivation. It is not a new problem. It has been recognized through the centuries. Knowing what is right does not always mean we will do what is right. Humans are not always capable of living up to their own best understanding of what is right or good. Why is this? I suggest there are three obstacles that stand in our way of acting so as to resolve the harm we are causing to our planet and to future human beings: (1) our biological nature, (2) our current culture, and (3) cosmic demoralization. These factors influence how we think and act, threaten to undermine our rational intentions, and thereby contribute to the peril of planet Earth.

The first obstacle is our biological nature. There is no good reason why we should expect that biological evolution has designed us to be motivated to act for the long term and the big picture. Individuals and ultimately species are selected by their relative rates of reproduction in particular environments. Genetically programmed motivators in our nervous systems, experienced as emotions, direct us to care for ourselves and our families, and to cooperate with others in small communities.[3] However, they are not sufficient by themselves to motivate us to care for all humans or the planet. From an evolutionary perspective, genetically programmed instincts, drives, and emotions need only equip us, or any species, to nourish and defend ourselves and our offspring to the point when the offspring reproduce. This means that in the past our view of the future has needed to be only short term. We have needed to project only cyclical patterns, following the seasons of the year, in order to hunt and gather our food or to produce that food domestically. We have needed to think ahead only a few decades to plan for the well-being of our own offspring. In their myths and rituals, many cultural traditions reflect these biological concerns with natural cycles of the year and with the human life cycle in kin groups. In stable environments, both natural and human cycles repeat over and over again. If we are biologically evolved to be concerned for others and our future in this limited way, how can we become motivated to act on behalf of the welfare of the entire planet for centuries to come? In short, our biology by itself has not equipped us for our new era of the global village.

Nor has our contemporary culture been adequate, even though cultures have extended our biological capacities. People such as geneticist Richard Dawkins, psychologist Donald Campbell, and philosopher-theologian Ralph Burhoe have recognized the limits of our biology to motivate us to act for the greater good.[4] They suggest that human culture exerts a second kind of influence on individual human beings. Social conditioning can stretch biological short-term concern for kin to concern for the welfare of others beyond the family. In the past, societies have built on and channeled biological motivations by encouraging generations of humans to think of city-states, nations, and religious communities as extended families, so that individuals come to identify their own good with that of a greater political-economic-social-religious system. Through cultural institutions, including religion, humans have stretched their biological motivation to care for close kin to the point that they sometimes even risk sacrificing their own well-being and that of their children for the greater, common good.

However, today our reigning political and economic systems, and much of our philosophical and religious thought reinforce individual selfishness and short-term interests at the expense of the greater good. Ironically, this reinforcement has not been brought about because of intentional human malevolence but because of our quest for greater good. Beginning with the American and French revolutions a few centuries ago and including late twentieth-century revolutions against communism in Eastern Europe, we have witnessed a decentralization of power and an emphasis on the rights of the individual in the Western world. This has been reinforced by the rise of free-market economies in which the creative imagination and technological inventiveness of individuals and businesses produce a supply of goods, and the decision making of each individual consumer provides the demand.

Correlated with this political and economic transformation, during the past few centuries we have seen the rise of the philosophy of atomistic individualism — the view that each individual person is complete unto him- or herself, that mind has greater worth than matter, that other creatures and the earth have only instrumental value for human welfare, and that right and wrong, good and bad are only expressions of individual motivations and desires. Most religious traditions that stress individual salvation or the care and cure of individual souls have not provided much help in thinking about the common good. Even when religion has manifested itself in a social gospel, such as in the civil rights and black power movements or in liberation theologies, the goal has usually been increasing opportunities for the good of human individuals.[5] As important as such a goal is, in our current political, economic, and philosophical climate, such a focus of value in the individual does not help stretch our biologically based selfish and kin-group interests. Thus, our culture is also an obstacle to our motivation to act for the long-term, planet-wide future. How then can we expect to become motivated to care about long-term ecological consequences? How then can we expect to become concerned about a global village in peril? We ourselves are the peril in the global village.

Many people, of course, are concerned with more than themselves. They have come to know about a bigger picture of an evolving universe, about how long it has taken to create life on Earth, about the long-term history of human civilizations, and about how rare and precious the earth, its inhabitants, and human cultures are. These often are people who are scientifically literate and are concerned about nuclear holocaust, burgeoning population growth, and wasteful consumerist economies. I have met many of them as students in my classes in environmental ethics and in world religions and the environment.

One problem they face, however, is demoralization. With an awareness of the emerging global village, they realize how complex things are. They wonder how much any one person can make a difference. They say, "Even if I do the right thing, will that really count?" This is one of the common questions from people who have developed a concern for future generations, other species of life, and the complex systems of our planet. They are grappling with the problem of becoming demoralized in the face of complexity.

A few of these people are aware of another element of this problem of demoralization. Demoralization can also become cosmic. I remember my first experience with "cosmic demoralization" several years ago. I was teaching a semester-long course in environmental ethics. About a week before the end of the course, and the school year, I read an article in the newsletter *Science Impact*, which was published under the auspices of the American Association for the Advancement of Science.[6] It was about mass extinctions due to accidents for which no biological evolution on Earth can prepare a species. It was about how the extinction of the dinosaurs had probably occurred sixty-six million years ago when an asteroid collided with the earth. The impact of the collision was large enough that for thousands of years the earth was ravaged with global firestorms, "nuclear winters," and mass extinctions — a global holocaust so great that, in comparison, anything I had read about possible human-caused disasters seemed insignificant. All this occurred through what David Raup calls "wanton evolution," a major shift in the "rules of the game" of life on Earth, which had no relation to the conditions of biological evolution up to that time.[7] The *Science Impact* article concluded that such a disaster could happen again with a high degree of probability.

Knowing about such occurrences and the fact that they could occur again was a difficult challenge as I completed my environmental ethics course that year. What good was it to teach students that we are part of the natural world, that there is inherent value in all life forms, that we should live in harmony with the nature that has created us? What good was it to teach all this when that same nature could destroy us just the way it had destroyed the dinosaurs? I was experiencing cosmic demoralization.

Of course, one can point out that prior mass extinctions led to a proliferation of new forms of life. The extinction of the dinosaurs made it possible for many smaller species of mammals to flourish as they had never been able to flourish before. One of these species gave rise to a line of evolution that has led to our own species, *Homo sapiens*. However, this fact does not solve the problem of cosmic demoralization, for a new asteroid collision or similar catastrophe could once again radically alter the earth and change the conditions for survival. If such an event occurs again, the new life might be something other than human life.

In light of the problem of demoralization, including cosmic demoralization, along with our biological and cultural shortsightedness, how can humans find fulfillment in a global village that we have placed in peril? How can we find the emotional strength and courage to live so that human civilization and life will flourish? How can we seek our own fulfillment and also live so as to sustain our planet, knowing that nature itself may not support our endeavors?

In response to these problems, the following chapters will explore some new ways of thinking. We will ask how new understandings of God and of ourselves might help us find meaning, moral guidance, and hope.

⮌ Chapter 4 ⮎

Sacred Centers

"What is sacred?" When Audrey Shenandoah asked this question of Onondaga children, they replied, "My mother." Shenandoah is an elder in the Onondaga Clan of the Iroquois federation. At a conference on "Spirit and Nature" she was interviewed by Bill Moyers for his video on the same subject.[1] Shenandoah had given a talk about her Native American beliefs and how they help motivate her people to care for the earth. In that talk she had spoken about how as a child she had learned to refer to the earth as mother. When Moyers asked why, she replied that it was a way of saying the earth was sacred.

Shenandoah asked the children what was sacred to them because she was trying to help them understand what the word "sacred" meant. Shenandoah then told Moyers that for children to regard their mothers as sacred meant that the mothers of these children were the centers of their being. That is why their mothers were sacred to them.

What does it mean to say that something is the center of our being? It means that our lives revolve around it. If we ask why our lives revolve around something, one reason might be that it is the source of our existence. It brought us into being and nurtures our growth and development. Mothers do these things. So do fathers and other primary people in our lives.

It is not surprising then that many people of the world, when they have thought about what brings them into being, have thought of the earth and its natural processes as if they were people. The creative and sustaining forces of nature are personified, because the relationship that human beings have with them is like the relationship people have with parents and other nurturing members of older generations. For Native Americans like Audrey Shenandoah, steeped in the traditions of her ancestors, if is quite easy to speak of the earth as mother and to also speak of the forces of nature with other personal terms.

Further, when Shenandoah asked the children in her community how they should treat their mothers, who were sacred to them, the children responded that they should care for their mothers. Just as their mothers cared for them, they should do the same. Extending this sense of responsibility to Mother Earth, Shenandoah added that Native Americans also understood themselves to have a responsibility to care for the earth.

I have suggested that a reason why human beings might regard the earth and natural forces as sacred is that they are the source of our being and our development. Another way of saying this is that sacred realities meet basic human needs: physical needs and also social and psychological needs.[2] Furthermore, when some needs are met, the status quo is maintained; when other needs are met, there is a transformation of individuals and societies to new states of being. Anthropologist Ward Goodenough suggests that religions function to both maintain and transform human selves.[3] As systems of self-maintenance and self-transformation, religions draw on multiple understandings or interpretations of the sacred, even within the same society. Because the needs of humans are so complex and also because of the varying conditions under which groups of humans have lived throughout history, the understanding of what is sacred is quite varied. The centers of people's lives are many, and even in one society the centers may shift so that there are many sacred centers, depending on exactly which needs are being met.

In the Vedic religion of ancient India, for example, many deities were understood to meet a variety of human needs. Ancient Indian poets created "praise-hymns" to sacred realities such as the Dawn, who each day responds to the basic need for light, and to Agni, the god of fire who provides warmth, energy for cooking food, and who in his smoke transmits sacrifices to other sky deities. However, among the main deities in the Rig-Veda, the collection of these hymns of praise, two stand out. One is Varuna and the other is Indra.

Unlike other Vedic deities who are often associated with the forces of the natural world, Varuna and Indra are more important for their involvement in social maintenance and transformation. Varuna, who lives in the vault of the sky, is the guardian of the social order. Making sure that people tell the truth and act in just ways, Varuna is understood to punish antisocial behavior and to uphold the authority of earthly kings. In contrast, Indra, who is often referred to in the Vedas as the chief of the gods, protects society from outside invaders. In doing so he is portrayed as amoral in Vedic mythology: He is "a lecherous youth and a drunken, boastful adult. After consuming offerings of thousands of buffalo and drinking lakes of intoxicants, Indra lurches off to war and there assists his people" from the threats of alien powers.[4] Sometimes Indra battles the demon of drought with the storms that bring life-giving rains. Sometimes he leads in warfare against human invaders. While Varuna works to maintain the status quo, Indra acts to counter society's disintegration from the threats of natural and social forces with the corresponding need for transformation.

In some societies the functions of Varuna and Indra are assumed by a single deity who is regarded as a divine ruler of the society and even of the natural world. The only god to be worshiped by the people of Israel as their creative and sustaining center is portrayed in the Hebrew Bible. Among many other things, Yahweh is a god of war who liberates his people from slavery to conquer the Promised Land. He also is a god who establishes the social order by giving his people the commandments they are to obey in response to their deliverance. Yahweh is thus both a sacred center of transformation that creates a society and a sustaining ruler that with the help of earthly surrogate rulers maintains the social order.

In human history there are many ways in which societies have understood the sacred realities that respond to basic human needs, that function both to maintain and to transform human life and also life in the rest of the natural world. I have given only a few. Such sacred realities provide centers around which people's lives have revolved and still revolve today. They are still credible and relevant in the ways of living for many people.

Yet many others like myself live and think in a world shaped by modern science, described in the second chapter. For me these ancient ways, while fascinating, are problematic as mental pictures of our world. While I may like the lessons for living they contain, such as preserving the earth, liberating oppressed peoples, and enabling social stability, I cannot accept them as the reasons for the way I should live — unless I can translate them into thinking that is compatible with contemporary science.

One problem I face is that many understandings of sacred centers seem too small for what we know about the universe today. While it is true that the earth is a source and sustainer of human life, to make the earth a sacred center does not take into account that it is an offspring, a child if you will, of the larger evolving universe. To say that Indra is the chief of the gods may mean that he is still important in certain life situations. But he is not chief in the sense of being the ultimate center from which all things come into being. Many traditional sacred centers are the centers for particular peoples in their particular geographical and historical circumstances. At one time they could be thought of as the center of the world. But the world has expanded from a flat Earth to the solar system, to the universe of billions of galaxies each containing billions of stars. In some way, a sacred center today has to be the center of the entire expanding universe as well as the center of our own lives. That is a big stretch for some traditional ideas.

One reason why many understandings of sacred centers are too small is that they are the results of human thought from a particular time and place. Such thinking draws on the ideas present in a particular culture. When one looks at all the cultures of the world, one finds a serious problem: the astonishing diversity of sacred realities. Anthropologist Anthony Wallace has estimated that there are more than one hundred thousand religions that have occurred throughout human history, from the tribal traditions of hunting-gathering societies to the great religions that began developing twenty-five hundred years ago in China, India, and the Middle East. Each of the great religions such as Hinduism, Buddhism, Judaism, Christianity, and Islam contains a variety of traditions.

This variety is to be respected and appreciated. Yet how can it be explained? Is there any way we can begin to account for it? One way to understand the diversity of religion and various conceptions of the sacred is to turn to contemporary science and outline two general features that seem to be crucial in an emerging scientific world view. These are naturalism and evolution. The modern scientific perspective holds that everything in the universe is ultimately comprised of energy-matter and information, and that the processes of change going on in the universe can be described in general evolutionary terms. From this starting point it is possible to outline the general history of the universe in such a way that religious diversity makes sense.

One of the primary characteristics of energy-matter is described by the second law of thermodynamics: the natural tendency of the universe is to move toward a state of random disorder. If this is a fundamental feature of the universe, how did more complex entities such as life and mind arise? Ilya Prigogine and others have wrestled with this problem in recent decades.[5] To resolve it, one can postulate that creation comes about through the interaction of chance and law. In the universe's fourteen-billion-year-history since the big bang, there seems to have been a tendency toward establishing new stabilities in nature. This process is essentially random, often without results, until a particular combination of positive and negative energy uncovers a new stable state, heretofore a "hidden" pattern contained in the informational ground of the universe, and a particular atom such as hydrogen is formed. The same random search for stable states continues as atoms form more complex arrangements called molecules, as molecules form still more complex stable arrangements that are self-reproducing and hence living, as living organisms discover new genetic patterns that allow them to diversify and adapt to, or become stable in, particular environments — until we humans appear on the scene. With our complex central nervous system marked by a highly developed outer brain layer called the neocortex, humans continue this process by creating new symbolic information patterns and weaving these together in what are called cultures.

Thus, according to the view of things suggested by evolutionary naturalism, as the energy-matter and information within the universe continually interacts with itself, it produces an almost infinite variety of structures. Many of these reproduce in ways that bring still greater variety of forms into being. To bring about diversity seems to be what the universe itself is engaged in doing.

Of course, not everything created exists for all time. On our own planet, space and time are finite. In order to have the continual creation of new forms of energy-matter, life, and even new forms of thought and behavior, some old patterns must die or be transformed. Creation involves death and transformation. As the environmentalist John Muir has written, "Nature is ever at work building and pulling down, creating and destroying, keeping everything whirling and flowing, allowing no rest but in rhythmical motion, chasing everything in endless song out of one beautiful form into another."[6]

This brief evolutionary-naturalistic picture helps us see how the variety of religions and their understandings of the sacred might be rooted in the very nature of things. Can this evolutionary picture help us live more effectively with the sacred? In later chapters I will suggest that it can help by developing the perspective of naturalistic theism, in which the sacred or divine is thought of as a system of nonpersonal processes within the natural world. For now, however, I would like to suggest that this evolutionary picture can help those who affirm a more traditional, personal view of God. How might the picture of creation I have developed be understood as expressing the "will of God"?

Arthur Peacocke, a biochemist and a theologian, suggests metaphorically how we might understand God's purpose in a pluralistic world. He suggests that God and creation might be portrayed in aesthetic terms. The universe is like a cosmic symphony with God as the composer and conductor. God,

> beginning with an arrangement of notes in an apparently simple tune, elaborates and expands it into a fugue by a variety of devices of fragmentation and reassociation; by turning it upside down and back to front; by overlapping these and other variations of it in a range of tonalities; by a profusion of patterns of sequences in time, with always the consequent interplay of sound flowing in an orderly way from the chosen initiating ploy.... In this kind of way might the creator

be imagined to unfold the potentialities of the universe he himself has given to it.[7]

If one includes in the universe not just inanimate and living forms, but also the various patterns of human behavior and experience, and of scientific thought and artistic expression — if one includes within the universe the various religions of the world and the diversity of ideas about the sacred — then we can regard all forms of cultural diversity, including religious diversity, as movements in the cosmic symphony composed and conducted by God. This is what God seems to be doing, which fits with our observations of diversity in our world today.

Of course, if one adopts this view of God as a cosmic composer and symphony conductor, one must give up the traditional idea of eternal, unchanging truth being expressed in any particular religion, even those religions claiming to have a special revelation. It means giving up the idea that only one religion can provide an adequate way of thinking and living. Religious thinkers of any one tradition must allow that other religions offer legitimate ways of providing meaning and moral direction for human living. In an evolutionary universe guided by a "master musician," all have to re-understand their faiths "not as the one and only, but as one of several."[8]

If the idea of eternal, unchanging truth is let go, then it is possible to have a concept of God, even a concept of a personal God, that complements the history of the universe portrayed by evolutionary naturalism. One can then see that the plurality of religions is the work of a continually creating God. This work comes to fruition in different ways in different times and places. Dynamic cultural pluralism is thus a part of a larger, dynamic, unfolding process of God's universal ongoing creation. Therefore, rather than diversity being a problem, it can be appreciated, lived with, rejoiced in. Human beings, regardless of which particular scientific or religious position they espouse at a particular time and place, can find meaning for their lives by regarding their particular, present standpoints as the result of divine creativity. They can find purpose for their lives by further participating in creative transformations of their own thoughts and of themselves. In an evolving universe, continual transformation in both major and minor ways is due to sacred creativity, and maintaining the status quo means continually adapting to new situations.

How can we portray this continual creative transformation of an evolving universe in a way that someone who thinks within the world view of modern science might find religiously meaningful? How can we develop a modern, naturalistic idea of our sacred center, the source, sustainer, and transformer of all existence? This is what I will attempt to do in the following chapters. Let's begin by reflecting on creative mystery.

❦ Chapter 5 ❧

Creative Mystery

One way to understand the great variety of ways in which the sacred has been portrayed is to recognize that all ideas about sacred centers, including the one developed in this book, are related to particular times and places, to the cultural symbols then available to human imagination. All these, even though quite different, are human attempts to comprehend the mystery that has created the world. This is not only recognized today. Ancient ways of thinking have also understood that the source of all existence, which sustains and transforms the world in all its forms, is more than humans can comprehend. It is mystery.

At the same time human beings have understood the sacred as something present in their midst. This must be so if basic human needs are to be met in relation to sacred centers. Both sacred mystery and sacred presence have shaped the ways humans have thought about the sacred. Using ideas that describe their own experience of themselves and their world, humans have created analogies to describe metaphorically the mysterious presence that works in the world continually to create and recreate aspects of the world, human society, and individual human life.

Both recognizing the mystery of the sacred and attempting to comprehend it are exemplified in the opening passage of the *Tao Te Ching* attributed to Lao Tzu: "The Tao than can be told is not the eternal Tao.... Nameless it is the origin of Heaven and earth; nameable, it is the mother of all things."[1] In the final analysis, the ultimate source of all existence is beyond words; it cannot be thought. It is mystery. However, it must be talked about in some way or other if humans are to understand and respond to it. So is it named with an analogy: like a mother, it gives birth to all things. Such a notion of motherhood does not necessarily imply that it is humanlike, a personal reality. The analogy is relational. We are related to the Tao like we are related to our mothers.

Another religious text that combines the idea of mystery with the creative working of the sacred is from one of the ancient Hindu scriptures, the Rig-Veda. This text tries to fathom the ultimate source of all existence in ways that recognize its otherness from all we know, and it also uses some elements of what we do know and understand to portray "That One Thing."

> There then was neither being (Sat) nor non-being (Asat):
> There was no air, nor firmament beyond it.
> Was their stirring? Where? Beneath what cover?
> Was there a great abyss of unplumbed water?
>
> There was not death nor anything immortal;
> Nor any sign dividing day from night.
> That One Thing, breathing no air, was yet self-breathing;
> No second thing existed whatsoever.
>
> Darkness was hidden in deeper darkness;
> This All was as a sea without dimensions;
> The Void still held unformed what was potential,
> Until the power of Warmth (tapas) produced the sole One.
>
> Then, in that One, Desire stirred into being,
> Desire that was the earliest seed of Spirit.
> (The sages probing in their hearts with wisdom
> Discovered being's kinship to non-being.
>
> Stretching their line across the void they pondered;
> Was aught above it, or was aught below it?)
> Bestowers of the seed were there; and powers;
> Free energy below; above, swift action.
>
> Who truly knows, and who can here declare it?
> Whence It was born, and how this world was fashioned?
> The gods came later than the earth's creation;
> Who knows then out of what the world has issued?

Whether the world was made or was self-made,
He knows with full assurance, he alone,
Who in the highest heaven guards and watches;
He knows indeed, but then, perhaps, he knows not![2]

This hymn recognizes that there must be an ultimate source of all existence but that it cannot be thought in our terms of existence or nonexistence; it is beyond our usual ways of thinking. No one knows how the world came into being, not even "He" in the highest heaven who should know everything. It is mystery. Yet, we have to say something. We might say it is a purely potential state. That state has power; it is self-breathing; it has warmth or energy, the capability for action; it has desire. As different as it is from humans, we still try to grasp what it is by thinking that it is analogous to what we humans feel within ourselves when we are stirred from within to act and create.

The analogy of mother in the *Tao Te Ching* is a relational metaphor. In a scientific age with a naturalistic understanding of things in nonpersonal terms, it may still be helpful to think of our relation to the mysterious creative source of existence in personal ways. However, the analogies in the hymn from the Rig-Veda go beyond relationships. They specify something about the inner state of "That One Thing" by saying that it was self-breathing and contained desire. Thus, "That One Thing" itself, not just our relationship to it, is vaguely portrayed in personal terms.

For many today, a problem with ancient ways of thinking about the sacred is that the analogies used to conceptualize mysterious creativity are often personal analogies. Insofar as these analogies are metaphors of relationship, they are not problematic. It is possible to describe a relationship to a nonperson in personal terms. Parental images can be used to talk about our relationship to the earth, or even to the universe as a whole. Humans and other forms of life on Earth are children of the workings of natural processes. It may still be helpful then to think of the earth as Mother or the God of Israel as Father if we understand these to be metaphors expressing our *relationship* with the earth or with an ultimate source of existence on which we are dependent. Furthermore, in overcoming the environmental peril in our global village, it may be important that we encourage the use of the relationships signified by personal metaphors to help motivate us to care for our planet.

Yet, usually the ancient ways of thinking take us beyond personal metaphors as metaphors of relationship. Often the metaphors are used to suggest that the divinities have an inner life that is personal. They have self-conscious intentionality. They can understand, plan, decide, and carry out their decisions analogous to the ways that humans understand, plan, decide, and carry out their decisions. Humans, therefore, can converse and commune with them in the same way that we converse and commune with other humans. Food can be ritually shared and prayers can be made to such sacred centers in the expectation that the sacred realities will respond. Such ritual communion and conversation, even in a scientific age, may help focus human activity for the benefit of other humans and the planet. However, when I take a scientific perspective, I cannot believe that the forces and processes of nature are personal in any human sense. For this reason, many of the ancient ways of thinking about the sacred seem incredible to me and others whose minds are shaped by scientific ways of thinking.

Sometimes even contemporary authors use personal inner states as analogies or metaphors to describe the mysterious creativity in the universe. One of the most powerful statements about creation I have read is by Nikos Kazantzakis, who describes the process of evolution as the result of a divine creative activity. He personifies this activity as a "Cry."

> Blowing through heaven and earth, and in our hearts and the heart of every living thing, is a gigantic breath — a great Cry — which we call God. Plant life wished to continue its motionless sleep next to stagnant waters, but the Cry leaped up within it and violently shook its roots: "Away, let go of the earth, walk!" Had the tree been able to think and judge, it would have cried, "I don't want to. What are you urging me to do? You are demanding the impossible!" But the Cry, without pity, kept shaking its roots and shouting, "Away, let go of the earth, walk!"

It shouted in this way for thousands of eons; and lo! as a result of desire and struggle, life escaped the motionless tree and was liberated.

Animals appear — worms — making themselves at home in water and mud. "We're just fine here," they said. "We have peace and security; we're not budging!"

But the terrible Cry hammered itself pitilessly into their loins. "Leave the mud, stand up, give birth to your betters!"

"We don't want to! We can't!"

"You can't, but I can. Stand up!"

And lo! after thousands of eons, man emerged, trembling on his still unsolid legs.

The human being is a centaur; his equine hoofs are planted in the ground, but his body from breast to head is worked on and tormented by the merciless Cry. He has been fighting, again for thousands of eons, to draw himself, like a sword, out of his animalistic scabbard. He is also fighting — and this is his new struggle — to draw himself out of his human scabbard. Man calls in despair. "Where can I go? I have reached the pinnacle, beyond is the abyss." And the Cry answers, "I am beyond. Stand up!" All things are centaurs. If this were not the case, the world would rot into inertness and sterility.[3]

This is powerful, poetic writing. But is the creative activity of the universe really a "cry"? Does evolution occur because of this inner torment? Do the desire and struggle humans feel in themselves offer the best analogy for how creation works in the universe? As powerful as the poetry is, as helpful as it might be in eliciting feelings that encourage us to resonate with the long, arduous processes of evolution, it does little to increase our understanding of how we have come to be and how we can further become.

Can we think about the sacred in ways that are consistent with the nonpersonal way of understanding things that is part of the scientific world view? I think so. Although personal ways of characterizing the sacred are more prevalent, if one looks at the cultures of the world, one still finds examples of the use of nonpersonal metaphors. I already have given one, the Tao or "Way of Heaven and

Earth." Another is the Melanesian concept of *mana*. *Mana* and parallel terms in other cultures (from some Native American societies to some African peoples) refer to the "experienced presence of a powerful but silent force in things or persons, especially any occult force which is believed to act of itself, as an addition to the forces naturally or usually present."[4] While a scientifically minded person will question the existence of occult forces as such, my point here is that it is an example of the sacred characterized as a power and not as a person. Even some of the metaphors in the Hebrew and Christian Bibles speak of God in nonpersonal terms. For example, the idea of spirit originally comes from the physical realm of wind and breath. Holy Spirit is not necessarily a designation of a personal divine being, although it is associated with other metaphors that portray God in personal terms.

The existence of nonpersonal metaphors for the sacred in traditional cultures can open us up to the possibility of using nonpersonal metaphors today to speak of whatever it is that continually creates the world and life, including human life. Contemporary theologian Gordon Kaufman does just that. For Kaufman, God is a symbol that helps us unify in our consciousness all the forces and processes of nature and history that create all living things and especially human beings, and that work to make humans more humane. Like many traditional views of the sacred, Kaufman's perspective recognizes that when we consider the creation of the world, we are ultimately confronted with mystery. Yet he goes on to talk about how the symbol God points to something working within the world. Kaufman calls this immanent aspect of the sacred "serendipitous creativity."[5] The name God, he writes, designates "that creativity, that mystery, which undergirds our human existence in all its complexity and all its diversity."[6]

Serendipitous creativity points to a system, the parts of which work together in unpredictable ways to create such things as new life, new truth, and new community. We can use the idea of serendipitous creativity to talk about the religious significance of biological evolution or of the birth and development of a single living organism. Various components come together in unpredictable ways to create a new species and also new individuals. For example, the interactions of our genes, our family environment, our wider society, and our natural world work together to make each of us a unique human being. All these parts working together create something of value, a particular living human organism.

We also can use the idea of serendipitous creativity to talk about progress in science. If one reads James Watson's book *The Double Helix*, one can see how serendipitous creativity describes a system of discovery in which such things as experimental facts, competing scientists, and human imagination interacted to give rise to the discovery of the structure of DNA.[7] No one fact, no one scientist, no one act of thought produced the discovery. Many of these coming together resulted in one of the major scientific discoveries of the twentieth century.

Serendipitous creativity is also a way of understanding how human communities are created. No human alone creates such communities. The interactions among humans and between humans and the natural world create communities in ways that cannot be planned or foreseen by any one individual. For example, Kaufman writes that the professional community of "modern science has certainly been a human creation, but no individual or group at the time of its origins in the seventeenth century had any notion of the complex institutional structures, modes of education and discipline, moral and communal commitments, financial and physical resources, not to say ways of thinking...which constitute science today."[8] The same is the case with modern democratic governments. No one person simply thought out and produced the complex political systems we have today. Many individuals contributed to their evolution over time, but no one could have planned or predicted their contemporary manifestations. It is the same with the building of cities. "Any modern city is the product of human planning and intention — every brick was laid by a deliberate human act — but no one simply decided modern London or New York or Tokyo would be a fine thing to build, worked out the plans, and then brought it into being."[9]

Serendipitous creativity is a contemporary, nonpersonal way of describing the ever present working of the sacred. Even as we recognize that all human descriptions, all metaphors, are acts of the human imagination that in the end fall short of allowing us to understand creative mystery, we still seek partial ways to comprehend the mother of all things. Serendipitous creativity is one such attempt. In the following chapters, I will suggest that this creativity can be thought of as a two-part process: one part gives rise to new variations in the cosmos, in life, and in human society; the other part selects and continues some of these new variations, which in turn contribute to further creation. My ideas too are only partial, only one way to think about God or the sacred for today. I recognize that I am gaining only a glimpse of the mysterious creativity that pervades the universe and the lives of each one of us. This mysterious creativity, which I partly understand, is my own sacred center in a scientific age.

❦ Chapter 6 ❧

To Err Is Divine

If one is used to thinking about God as a being who created the world, trying to think about God as a process or event of creation may seem quite radical. When I began to reflect on God as a process of creation, I found it helpful to come up with unusual expressions that heightened my sense of what this process could be in our daily lives. This chapter explores one unusual expression — to err is divine.

An immediate reaction to this might be, "That's a mistake." I agree. The usual saying is "To err is human, to forgive divine." However, my mistake highlights the main point I wish to raise. I am suggesting that when we think of God as a process of creation, one aspect of that process is, we might say, mistake making — error making.

How can God be regarded as mistake making? Affirming this is indeed a mistake from the perspective of the way we usually talk about God — that is, from the way things are said traditionally. However, if we understand what an error or mistake is, we might make sense of this unusual expression. "Error" or "mistake" can mean a deviation from the way things have usually been said or done. These words signify mis-takes, so that the past is not reproduced in exactly the same way. Yet, from another perspective, mis-takes are new variations on the past; therefore, they may possibly be a creative advance into the future.[1]

However, even if we acknowledge that mistakes are possible creative advances, why bring God into the picture? Why not just talk about human creativity? Let me begin by saying that one reason I want to talk about God is that I'm a pragmatist. Following Charles Sanders Peirce I want to take abstract ideas and make them concrete; I want to define even words such as God, the ultimate source of existence, in a way that I can observe God working in the world. Many today have lost the capacity to talk about the sacred in such a way that the sacred or the divine is close to us. The ancients seemed to be able to sense God in their midst, but in our scientific age, when we do talk about God, some people place God as the originator of the big bang, that which gave the universe its initial impulse, and then they leave it at that. The source of all existence becomes a source only at the beginning of the universe and not a source of new forms of existence on our planet, in human history, and in our daily lives. God thus becomes like an absentee landlord, or a developer that leaves the scene. Religiously, that is no God at all.

Such a portrayal of the ultimate source of all things only at the beginning of the universe is an inadequate theology if that is all that can be said, because most religious traditions have been able to speak of the divine in their midst, in the ongoing workings of the world. They understand the sacred as an ever present source of individual and social maintenance and transformation. Thus, traditional religion and American pragmatic philosophy join to reinforce one of the central concerns expressed in this book, namely that God not be thought of only as a cosmic originator but also as a continual presence to which we can relate here and now and, in this relationship, find meaning and purpose for our lives.

As long as we think of God as some kind of being, we will have difficulty perceiving God in the midst of our lives. We imply that God is some kind of being when we use the word "God" as a noun and say God is the creator. However, if we think of the word "God" more as a verb (is this another mistake?) then we can say that God equals creating; God is the process of creation, the event of creation. A process of creation, a particular pattern that makes up the structure of creating as it takes place — this we can possibly observe in our midst. Furthermore, if we understand the pattern that is the structure of creating, then we too can participate more intentionally and completely in the creative process. We can become more closely related to God.

When we specify the pattern of the creative process, we must recognize that we are only stating our ideas of it. Like all ideas, ideas about how creation takes place must be tested against further experiences of creativity in our midst. One possible idea about the pattern of creating that seems to fit much of experience is the idea proposed by Charles Darwin, namely that creating consists of two unrelated processes: one is the set of interactions that creates new variations; the other is the set of interactions that selects and preserves some variations over others. Darwin developed his theory of random variation and natural selection to account for the biological creation of new species. I think that his idea of how creating takes place can be extended to include creating in human cultures.

One part of this Darwinian pattern of creating is the occurrence of random variations. From the point of view of the past, of what has gone before, new variations are mistakes. Hence it is possible to say "To err is divine" and by this mistake in language capture one aspect of God as the process of creating at work in our midst.

Errors are a part of creating in the biological realm. Jacob Bronowski writes, "Life is a process of accurate copying.... [It] is also and essentially an evolutionary process, which moves forward only because there are errors in the copy, and every so often one of these errors is successful enough to be incorporated as another step or threshold in its progression."[2] Of course, not all errors in the chains of DNA that make up the genetic code lead to viable organisms. The vast majority do not. However, those errors that are not detrimental to the organism, that can be carried as a part of a modified genetic heritage and passed on to future generations, form the potential bases of a new species. Biological creation takes place by making mistakes.

The same thing occurs as part of the evolution of human culture, of human thought in science and art. What is different from the making of mistakes in biology is that the mistakes made by great thinkers and artists are often, though not always, intentional mistakes. In mathematics, for example, the inherited tradition from Euclid held to the postulate of parallel lines, that in the same plane two parallel lines never intersect. This two-millennia-old idea was challenged by some nineteenth-century geometers. We might say a mistake was made; there was a variation from the past and new non-Euclidian geometries were born. In some respects, these new non-Euclidian geometries were more accurate than the old in their application to the physical world, for example, to the world conceived by Albert Einstein's general theory of relativity.

Einstein himself made an intentional "copying error" in developing his theories of relativity. In arriving at the special theory of relativity, he denied the theorem of addition of velocities employed in classical physics. In a thought experiment to illustrate this theorem, Einstein imagined that a beam of light was projected from a fast moving train and another beam was projected from a stationary point along the track. According to the theorem of addition of velocities, a person at the stationary point could calculate the velocity of the beam from the train by adding the velocity of the moving train to that of the speed of light. Thus, from the reference frame of a stationary observer, light given off from a fast moving object achieves a greater velocity than light projected from a stationary object. Einstein denied this theorem of addition of velocities and held that the velocity of light (in a vacuum) always remains constant, regardless of the frame of reference of the observer. Based on this "mistake," this not repeating the tradition in physics, Einstein constructed the special theory of relativity.[3] Making mistakes or copying errors is one aspect of the creative process in culture as well as in biological evolution.

Intentional error making occurs in the arts as well as in science. A colleague of mine at Rollins College once said as we discussed the creative process: "Poets use words wrong."[4] Think of this statement itself for a second. After realizing how it also was a mistake, I set out to find examples of poets using words incorrectly. I can't say that all poetry exemplifies verbal copying errors, but the following one certainly does. In it the poet calls moonlight "stuff." This stuff, moonlight, runs. To make matters worse, the poet says that sand "laps"; usually waves lap against a sandy shoreline. There also is a wave line that has a "creep" in it; creep in this context is usually a verb. Furthermore, this wave line belongs to a pond that is a flower, a pansy. And Carl Sandburg calls his poem "Nocturne in a Deserted Brickyard." Here is the creative result of all these mistakes.

Stuff of the moon
Runs on the lapping sand
Out to the longest shadows.
Under the curving willows,
And round the creep of the wave line
Fluxions of yellow and dusk on the waters
Make a wide dreaming pansy of an old pond
In the night.[5]

To err is divine.

In these examples from science and poetry not only were mistakes made, but the maker refused to correct them. No doubt many new variations in science and art fail the tests making up their cultural environments, which are largely determined by the traditional ways of thinking and acting. Yet, others meet some of the established tests while at the same time they begin to reshape what constitutes acceptable criteria for good science or good art. One who makes mistakes and refuses to correct them may be harshly judged, but that person may also pave the way for a new movement in science, in art, or even in religion.

Salvador Dali is a striking example of the kind of artist I have in mind. Preoccupied with time, bending watches out of shape, he established new ways of seeing reality, called surrealism. What Einstein did in altering the thinking about reality in physics, Dali and artists like him were doing in late nineteenth- and in twentieth-century movements and schools in art.

A classic example of one who made mistakes, who refused to correct them, who was harshly judged by the standards of his cultural environment, and yet who prevailed to establish a major new cultural reality was Jesus of Nazareth. The Gospels of the Christian New Testament contain many stories about how Jesus came into conflict with some of the religious leaders of his day. Some of these leaders, the Pharisees, were holding rigorously to the standards of their religious tradition in an effort to revitalize their religion and their life. Jesus, however, is reported to have made mistake after mistake, thereby challenging interpretations of the established religious and moral code. For example, in violation of Sabbath regulations he allowed his followers to pick corn on this holy day of rest. He then compounded his error by proclaiming, "The Sabbath was made for humankind, not humankind for the Sabbath."[6] He went about sharing his life and love with those who were despised by religious authorities for not practicing the commandments. When he was challenged for eating with sinners, Jesus replied, "Those who are well have no need of a physician, but those who are sick; I have come to call not the righteous but sinners."[7]

Underlying these mistakes, indeed implied in them, was something that was an even greater error. Jesus seemed to speak in a manner, with an authority, that suggested he had an immediate and intimate relationship with the sacred source of all existence. He referred to this source with the Aramaic word *Abba* — an intimate address of a child to his father. We might translate *Abba* as "Daddy."[8] Such intimacy with the divine, not requiring the mediation of the moral and ritual law, was too much of a deviation from the old traditions. The cultural environment in which Jesus was operating did not have a niche, a "room for him in the inn." That environment was, of course, in the minds of his contemporaries who were in power, and they rejected him and his way, so they thought, by crucifixion.

Yet the mistakes Jesus made did not go away. Even though his closest followers turned away at his death, still the copying errors had taken root in the hearts and minds of those who had come to know him. His followers began to experience his character in their midst as they talked about having the "mind of Christ."

Perhaps we can understand Jesus' intimacy with God, if we remember that God as the source of all existence — physical, biological, societal — is the creative process working in our midst. As an aspect of that process, making his mistakes, Jesus was part of something far greater than himself as a human being. What he initiated with his mistakes was a more intimate understanding of how one can be related to ultimacy. This understanding has survived his relatively short human life span, because God as the creative event works in religion just as in art and in science. The copying errors generated in individual human minds are transmitted to other minds and sometimes bring about major reorganizations of the thought and practice in people's lives.

To many readers, it will seem that I have made many mistakes; I have not said things the way they have been said in the past. Are these mistakes mutations in religious thought that ought to be destroyed or might they be something else, a new and helpful way of portraying the sacred? That will be determined not by what I am saying. It will be determined only by how you and others respond, by whether these ideas help you make sense of your own experience in living. In terms of thinking about the sacred as the creative process, the way you and others respond to my thoughts is a part of the selection process operating in our culture as that culture is reflected in your own ways of thinking.

This selecting process is also an aspect of the creative process. On the one hand, mistake making is a part of that process and by not being afraid to make mistakes we become related to God working in our midst. On the other hand, selecting and retaining some mistakes while weeding out others is also something in which we humans participate. Here also we are intimately bound up with the sacred — in this case with judgment. To err is divine; to judge is divine. In the ongoing evolution of our own culture, our creating new variations and then critiquing and evaluating them makes us, like Jesus and his followers, children of God. We are intimate offspring of the ultimate source of all being as we carry on the work of the sacred creative reality that is the evolving of the universe.

✧ Chapter 7 ✧

Darwin and
the Dance of Tao

One of the most interesting concepts in ancient Chinese thought is the concept of *wu wei*, sometimes translated as "actionless action." The following is an expression of *wu wei* in the *Tao Te Ching*:

Under heaven nothing is more soft and yielding than water.
Yet for attacking the solid and strong, nothing is better;
It has no equal.
The weak can overcome the strong;
The supple can overcome the stiff.[1]

This passage illustrates the idea that the key to power and success is not to try so hard to overcome obstacles. Instead, like water one should simply "flow," seeking the path of least resistance, living in harmony with the Tao, the "Way of Heaven and Earth." Today we might say *wu wei* means living in harmony with the laws of nature or the way nature works.

Some time ago I gained a little more insight into actionless action as a result of some phone conversations with a friend. I had not spoken with this person for several years, but with one phone call it seemed like we just picked up where we left off. The conversation flowed with remarkable ease. We were both surprised how easy it was to talk — and talk we did, for hours, with no effort. It all just seemed to flow.

Thinking back on that conversation, I discovered why it flowed so easily. It was because neither one of us was trying to accomplish anything. We had no goal to realize — except one, simply to talk with each other. Thus, each of us was fully focused on the conversa-

45

tion itself and on one another. The result was like water winding its natural course in a stream — sometimes bubbling with excitement, sometimes flowing quietly in deep patterns of our minds.

When I spoke with another friend about that conversation, I received the response, "You were dancing." Dancing! What an interesting way to look at human relationships.

The primary challenge of dancing revolves around the question of who leads. I've had experiences, miserable experiences, of dancing when both of us were trying to lead. I also remember conversations that went much the same way. And I suspect there are human relationships — even long-term relationships — in which both parties try to control the relationship for their own purposes. When this happens, the relationship is likely to be a struggle. Each person is continually stepping on the other's toes.

Dancing and relationships work more easily when there is only one person leading. One person is thus in control, accomplishing his or her goals, while the other follows. That may work fine for ballroom dancing; in fact, it's the way it is supposed to go. However, in the dance of life, dancing with one person leading, one person in control and the other only following, can result in domination and dependence.

The best kind of dancing is when no one leads, when the leading is a back and forth sharing, when each party responds to the subtle movements, touches, gestures, and words of the other. When this happens both parties give themselves fully to the dance of dynamic relating. Then the relationship becomes a beautifully flowing movement of two people interacting with one another. Over time this can create beautiful patterns of creative friendship, partnership, and marriage. The key to this kind of zestful living is that neither participant is trying to advance his or her private goals. There is, in fact, no goal except the dance itself, being together in living life.

Dancing with no one leading, with no goal or purpose but the dance itself, is a good metaphor for portraying our contemporary scientific understanding of evolution on our planet. If one follows strictly the philosophical implications of neo-Darwinian theory, there is no overall purpose to evolution. The "copying errors" that modify species and bring new species into being are not part of any grand design. They are simply due to the continual interactions taking place within the cells of organisms. These genetic variations are translated into modified structures and behaviors of the organism. This organism then further interacts with its surrounding environment as it seeks to feed, defend, and reproduce itself. Depending on how successful it is in doing these things, it continues its re-formed genetic line.

The point is that there are two distinct kinds of processes. One produces changes in the DNA, in the genes at the molecular level in the germ cells of the organism. The other process occurs at the level of the entire organism, between the organism and other plants, animals, and more general conditions such as climate in its environment. The fact that these two kinds of processes are not coupled together as one single process is the reason why there is no purpose other than the activities of variation and selection. For this reason, some say evolution is opportunistic: whatever changes occur at the molecular level may or may not happen to fit the then existing environment, which itself consists of other living and nonliving forms that are also constantly changing. But I prefer the image of the dance. Darwinian evolution portrays nature as constantly dancing — dancing with no one leading but with all participating and mutually influencing one another.

To say there is no overall purpose in evolving nature is not to say there are no laws. Part of what determines the success of any variation in the genes is that those variations and the resulting changes in the complete organism still obey the laws of physics and chemistry. Similarly, when two people are conversing in a way that simply flows, with the only purpose being the conversation, there are still the rules of the language being spoken. And dances, even dances with no one leading, still follow "rules" implied in the rhythms of music and of the particular type of dancing.

Nevertheless, even with the laws of nature, of language, of the dance, when one is in the interactions there is spontaneity. There is the opportunity to improvise, to "go with the flow." And like the flow of a river within its banks, this improvisational flowing within the laws of nature and society is what makes our lives and the world in which we live a creative, evolutionary world.

In religious thought, this creativity that continually gives rise to new structures, new life forms, new thoughts and practices in a society, can be called the "dance of God." A personalistic, theistic version of this idea is presented by Denise and John Carmody in their book *Christianity: An Introduction*. They suggest how effective people can become when they stop trying to control their actions and learn to dance with God.

> There is a tantalizing dictum from Christian tradition that puts the covenantal relationship between creator and creatures in the form of a practical maxim. "Act as though everything depended on God and pray as though everything depended on yourself." This maxim is so contrary to most Americans' expectations that frequently they invert it. Surely action, they reason, is our human affair, and prayer is where God comes in. But deeper Christian instinct confounds many other aspects of contemporary Western culture. To the Christian, the priority in all that we observe or do belongs to God the creator, the conserver, the concurer. She is the first cause and the final cause comprehensively.
>
> When people really believe this, Christians assert, their action or work or doing straightens out. Like runners who have learned about stretching, they move easily, with fewer tightnesses and cramps. Like people who have appropriated a trust walk, making it something adult, they let themselves go, expecting that God will catch them when they fall. The results are often impressive. In contrast to the "Type A" behavior of the stereotypic American executive, tight-jawed and hell-bent for a coronary, those who feel God's presence keep their work in perspective, taking cues from the subtle initiatives that a given situation offers. Because they are not pushing, they can receive such initiatives, take in the delicate signs that nature or other people give of how things are flowing. Because their egos are not blocking their horizon, they can move their bodies and minds dexterously. So they resemble a realized Zen master, who has no self and can follow Buddha-nature's flow. So they conjure up T. S. Eliot, who set the still point of union

with God in the context of a reality that was a dance. "Dance with me," the Christian God says. "Follow my lead, my music of the spheres."[2]

The Carmodys see "the subtle initiatives a given situation offers ... the delicate signs that nature or other people give of how things are flowing," as ultimately cues from a personal God, spoken of, even if only metaphorically, as some kind of being. I have reservations, however, about such views of the sacred in an age of science. As one who wishes to think theologically within the world view of science, I want to be able to test ideas about God empirically, that is, against something observable. Can one observe God? I think so, if one considers the cues themselves as part of the creative process, if one recognizes that the kind of interaction of which the Carmodys speak is itself the divine. Then we don't need to say "Dance with me" or "Follow my lead, my music of the spheres." The invitation needs only to be "Come dance." God *is* the music. Responding only to this brings one into relation with our sacred center.

Simply to dance, with the awareness that one is part of the divine "dance of nature" means that we are expressing a naturalistic view concerning the character of the sacred. Such a view seems to correspond with the Taoist understanding that, even if it cannot be described in its final or absolute state, there is nonetheless a Way of Heaven and Earth that is like a dance, a dance of nature in which we participate with no one leading. The dance just flows, like water, rock, and shoreline interacting according to the underlying laws of nature. The dance becomes *wu wei*, actionless action.

For some, dancing just for the sake of dancing, living just for the sake of living, will not seem sufficient. They will want to know what the payoff is. If the dance — or life — is going nowhere in particular, what is the goal, the purpose of it all? I suggest that there is no purpose or payoff in terms of fulfilling projected personal interests. This is because in the dancing, in the interactions with others and the world, our interests and purposes are often transformed. For the person who wants only to further existing desires, for the person who is not open to being changed, there is no payoff in dancing with no one leading.

However, for those willing to be transformed by the dance, there are payoffs. People who are willing to give themselves to dancing with the sacred, to flowing with the Tao, are likely to be more open and accepting of nature in all its fullness and all its changes. Hence they are more likely to regard other forms of life as valuable, even when the forms are always changing as a part of the ever creative dance. Similarly, they might be more accepting of other people as they are. To dance with no one leading means to be open to the subtle cues and initiatives from others. One can only be open if one trusts, respects, and even loves others for who they really are.

But the biggest payoff is for each of us as individuals. It is the payoff of participating fully in every moment of life. Of course many of us have goals we are trying to achieve, purposes we are trying to fulfill. We are thus looking toward the future, toward trying to better ourselves, our society, the world in which we live. This may be important as long as we are not too set in our ways, in our beliefs as to what actually will make things better. If we become too sure of what is good for us and our world, we will continue to create new problems that put ourselves and our planetary global village in peril. But we may also put ourselves in peril. If we are not open to our goals and ideals becoming transformed by the grace of the dance, we may miss out on the joy of being in relationship with the divine in our midst.

Haven't you ever wondered, as I have when I constantly strain at trying to get somewhere, whether or not we are missing something? Something important? Matthew Arnold puts it this way in a haunting poem, which some churches sing as a hymn:

> Calm soul of all things, make it mine
> To feel amid the city's jar,
> That there abides a peace of thine
> I did not make and cannot mar.
> The will to neither strive nor cry,
> The power to feel with others, give.
> Calm, calm me more; nor let me die
> Before I have begun to live.[3]

"Before I have begun to live!" That concerns me! In a life and a society always on the go, always trying to get somewhere else, is it possible that we could actually miss living? By not letting go to dance with others fully in the present, could we not die before we have begun to live?

In learning to dance with the natural world around us and with other human beings, we become more alive. This is the big payoff. We become more in tune with ourselves, others, and the natural world. We see more, experience more, enjoy more. We become part of the dance of the sacred — the dance of that system of interactions in the universe and society that brought us into being, that sustains us in our living, and that continually transforms us as part of the ever changing future.

Carmody and Carmody portray this creative system with the metaphor of personalistic theism. But Darwinism and Taoism suggest that the interactions in nature which just happen, or in human relations when no one leads — these interactions are the dance. They are the way — the Tao. They themselves are God. "Come dance with Me" says God personally conceived. Darwinism and Taoism simply say, "Come dance!"

✐ Chapter 8 ✎

Divine Dynamics:
Spirit and Word

A part of thinking about the sacred in a scientific age is responding to the question: "On what grounds does one establish that there is correspondence between some religious and some scientific concepts?" Many think that scientific and theological ideas cannot correspond because they belong to different realms of discourse. If they do, does this mean they cannot be related to one another? If we regard ideas as tools to help us get around in the world, we might say that the sciences and various religions offer different maps of the same world.

Compare in your mind two different kinds of maps of the same city. One is a street map; the other a subway map. The maps are quite different in many respects. Lines indicating routes rarely match up if one map is overlaid on the other. One map may include more territory that the other. Further, for some unknown reason each map has names different from those of the other. In spite of these differences, we have reason to assume that the maps are indeed of the same city. How can we support this assumption? We can use both maps in traveling around the city to see if there is a common set of street corners and subway stops. If there is, we can conclude that they are indeed maps of the same territory even though they appear quite different.

Something like this can be done with religious and scientific ideas. We assume they are maps of the same world, even though they are quite different and may even map different aspects of that world. Still, we should be able to find some points at which their ideas come together. If we use them to orient us on our life journeys in this world, we should find some points where some subway stops of one, say our scientific map, are congruent with some street corners of our religious map. They bring us to some of the same points. In this chapter I will suggest that concepts of *spirit* and *word* in the Christian map bring us to the same points as concepts from the science of nonequilibrium thermodynamics.

Nonequilibrium thermodynamics is the study of how more complex stable states arise out of less complex states, according to random fluctuations and inherent laws. In *From Being to Becoming*, Ilya Prigogine explains how contemporary nonequilibrium thermodynamics deals with irreversible processes.[1] These are temporal processes flowing in only one direction. They are found in open systems, that is, in systems that take in energy from outside of themselves to maintain their ordered states. When that energy increases they can evolve into more complex structures.

One example is Henri Bénard's classic study in 1900. A. Katchalsky gives a summary of Bénard's experiment and its interpretation by Lord Rayleigh.[2] He writes that Bénard

> kept a heavy liquid in a shallow dish which was carefully heated at the bottom.... He found that at a critical temperature, an instability set in and rings appeared near the wall of the dish. These rings, indicating cylindrical tubules in the liquid, increased in number and moved toward the center, filling up the whole volume with a honeycomb structure. On further heating, the Bénard structure disappeared, indicating that its existence is limited by a lower and upper boundary. The interpretation of the Bénard phenomenon was given in 1916 by ... Lord Rayleigh, who recognized that the pattern is due to the interaction of two flows: the heating of the bottom of the dish establishes an upward heat flow which tries to *destabilize* the system; but since the liquid at the hotter bottom of the dish has a lower density than the liquid at the cooler surface, a convection current arises which attempts to stabilize the behavior and to moderate the effect of the heat flow. Indeed, each volume cylinder, seen as a circle in the surface of the honeycomb structure, represents a flow of circulation....

that moves up and down each of the cylindrical tubules. This flow is what creates the tubular structure when viewed from the side and the honeycomb structure when viewed from the top.

The kind of interaction taking place in the Bénard experiment is described by Katchalsky as owing to "coupled non-linear flows." The energy from outside the system, the heat on the dish, does not simply flow in one direction through the liquid but sets up a reverse flow process, because of the relation between temperature and density. Heating up the dish sets up a set of fluctuations in the liquid that are at first random. However, after the fluctuations reach a particular point, laws of the relation of temperature and density go into effect and stabilize the interactions into the nonlinear flows, the flows circulating up and down each tubule. The movement of the liquid from its initial state to a new, more complex state occurs because of both the random fluctuations and the underlying laws of nature.

In *From Being to Becoming*, Prigogine gives several examples of creation taking place in this manner, not only at the physical level of existence but also at the chemical, biological, and even ecological levels of human populations. That which initiates the process varies from the heating of a liquid in the Bénard experiment, to catalysts in chemical reactions, to the addition of economic variables that rearrange human population. However, the process always seems to have two fundamental aspects — fluctuations that are initially stochastic or random, and hidden variables that determine the emerging new order.

For example, following the work of Peter Allen, Prigogine presents a computerized model of the possible "history" of urbanization of an initially uniform region. The uniform region of human population is analogous to the uniform distribution of molecules in a fluid prior to the Bénard instability. When four economic functions are introduced at each point in a network of fifty localities in this region, one begins to observe a set of fluctuations in population that leads to a new pattern of organization within the region. The new pattern matches remarkably well some of the actual populations in urban regions. Prigogine comments that "the final result depends in a complex manner on the interplay of deterministic economic laws and the probabilistic succession of fluctuations."[3] It is this interplay of chance disturbances and law that gives rise to new order.

Based on the work in nonequilibrium thermodynamics and other scientific work regarding evolutionary theory, it is possible to generalize a pattern of creativity characterized by two sets of processes. One set introduces new variations, random fluctuations in existing systems. The other involves inherent laws of nature that operate on the fluctuations to allow the development of new stable structures. We can hypothesize that such a pattern of creativity is present in the origins of the universe, in order to solve an interesting problem. As a result of the big bang some fourteen billion years ago, the universe began to expand, analogous to the way the surface of a balloon expands when blown up. The questions are, why does the universe not just expand uniformly in all directions until its density decreases and its temperature cools down to a few degrees above absolute zero? Why is anything at all created out of the initial inflation called the big bang?

It appears one must assume that two things are present along with the potential energy released in the initial inflation. First, there must be laws governing the formation of structures, so that, as the universe begins to cool, radiation forms elementary particles. Second, to prevent these elementary particles from simply expanding uniformly in all directions, one must assume fluctuations or disturbances that disrupt homogeneity. Cosmologist Joan Centrella suggests that "the soup of particles in the early universe was rippled with waves, much like the ocean."[4] As these waves moved through the early universe, they caused matter to squeeze together until it collapsed to form super clusters, galaxies, and stars.

Astrophysicist Eric Chaisson illustrates how this dual pattern of chance fluctuations and natural laws may have worked together to form galaxies. "Though probably distributed uniformly at first, matter, if left alone tends to coagulate inhomogeneously. This is because a uniform, unbounded, self-gravitating medium is basically unstable and eventually will fragment into individual pockets of matter. Some of these statistical fluctuations will disperse, but others will grow, especially in the presence of turbulence that was surely there in the early universe."[5] Along with the initial fluctuations and the turbulence that initially create pockets of hydrogen and helium atoms, laws of gravity, temperature, and density are at work. Some areas of matter coagulate and continue to grow as gravity attracts still more atoms. If enough mass accumulates — "at least one hundred billion times the mass of our Sun — a reasonably warm condensation will contract gravitationally, rotate a little, heat up, radiate energy, contract some more, rotate a little faster, and so on in this cyclical fashion until an equilibrium is achieved between the inward pull of gravity and the outward forces of rotation. In this way it is thought that all galaxies were formed in the first few billion years after the bang."[6]

Within galaxies this process of creation repeats itself. Chaisson goes on to point out that "pockets of gas form, also almost by accident, via statistical fluctuation, much as for galaxies...."[7] If the number of hydrogen atoms in such a pocket of gas is sufficiently large, as the interstellar gas cloud collapses under the influence of gravity, it will begin to heat up due to the friction resulting from the collision of hydrogen atoms until it reaches a point at which it ignites in nuclear fusion. The fusion of hydrogen to helium releases enormous amounts of energy. Some of this energy from one star, our Sun, is potential energy for the earth. It helps create and maintain physical, chemical, biological, social, and even mental processes, as Prigogine and others describe.

When one looks at the history of the universe in terms of the scientific mapping of the process of creation through random fluctuations and natural law, one realizes that this pattern of continual creation gives rise to a wondrous proliferation of diverse forms of matter, life, society, and mind. In his concluding remarks to a chapter titled "Self-Organization," Prigogine notes that

> there are no limits to structural stability. Every system may present instabilities when suitable perturbations are introduced. Therefore, there can be no end to history. Ramon Margalef has, in a beautiful presentation, described what he calls the "baroque of the natural world." He means that ecosystems contain many more species than would be "necessary" if biological efficiency alone were an organizing principle.

This "overcreativity" of nature emerges naturally from the type of description suggested here, in which "mutations" and "innovations" occur stochastically and are integrated into the system by the deterministic relations prevailing at the moment. Thus we have in this perspective the constant generation of "new types" and "new ideas" that may be incorporated into the structure of the system, causing its continual evolution.[8]

In the work of Prigogine, Chaisson, and others, one can see that a scientific map of creation in the universe involves two kinds of processes. The first is random fluctuations or disturbances of existing states of the universe; the second is the formation of new structures out of these disturbed states according to inherent laws. We might say that a disordering of a previous state on certain occasions and under certain conditions gives rise to new order.[9]

In there anything comparable in a religious map of creation in the universe? I suspect that one can make effective comparisons between ideas about creation in many religious traditions and those of modern science.[10] I see such a comparison in the conceptual map that can be drawn from Judaism and Christianity in which creation takes place by Spirit and Word.

The primary creation story of the Jewish and Christian traditions is Genesis 1. In the opening verses, the original state of creation is portrayed as a formless, watery void. It is a state of no-thingness, a state in equilibrium but with potential for all kinds of things. Creation itself begins when the Spirit of God moves over the face of the waters.

In the biblical tradition, the Hebrew word for spirit, *ruach*, has a complex set of meanings. According to the *Hastings Encyclopedia for Religion and Ethics*, it can be used physically, physiologically, psychically, and supernaturally or extra-humanly.[11] It signifies the wind in all its phases; the breath of humans, which is related to the life and energy of the body; heightened human emotions; and the work of extra-human agencies that affect humanity for good or ill. In most of these understandings of *ruach*, it seems that the Spirit of God is related to that kind of energy or force which on the one hand sustains life and on the other hand disturbs an existing state of affairs. In terms of our idea of scientific and religious maps, there is a conjunction of a subway stop and a street corner. In Genesis, when the Spirit or wind of God moves over the waters, it creates the same kind of disturbance from equilibrium that fluctuations and turbulence created in the formation of galaxies. Furthermore, the work of the Spirit never ends. The biblical God is involved in ongoing creation in nature and history. The Spirit blows where it wills, like the ongoing random fluctuations described by Prigogine and Chaisson. Creation involves continual disturbances in existing systems so that new stable states can emerge — new material elements, new forms of life, new developments in society, new patterns of thought. Spirit or random fluctuation is one part of divine dynamics.

However, in both maps disturbances of existing states are only the beginning of creative activity. What is needed to complete a particular instance of creation are the laws of the universe at its various levels of existence. According to the hidden laws of nature some random fluctuations are able to evolve to new states of equilibrium. In the Judeo-Christian map, this second aspect of divine dynamics is signified by the Word of God.

In the Bible, the notion of Word of God is based on a personal model of God, according to which the divine creator speaks out the creation. When one looks at what happens when God speaks in the opening chapter of Genesis, one sees that God's word is what brings order to the universe. Perhaps because of this, early Christian thinkers were able to develop a view of a cosmic Christ as the Word of God. This view is based on the meaning of the Greek word *logos*. "In the beginning was the *logos*, and the *logos* was with God and the *logos* was God."[12] For Greek-speaking thinkers, philosophers such as the Stoics and Platonists, *logos* signified not only word but also the reason of the universe.

Thus some Christian thinkers were able to interpret the Word of God, in the beginning with God and through whom all things were made, as the underlying order of the universe. Here again we have congruence between a scientific subway stop and a religious street corner. The Word represents the underlying laws that govern the evolution of the universe, so that when the Spirit blows were it wills, randomly creating fluctuations, new stable states and new levels of existence come into being. These states and levels in turn provide a basis for further divine dynamics. The activity of Spirit and Word is continuous. It is one way of speaking about the sacred as the ever present ground of all becoming.

What does this imply for how we live our lives? In the two previous chapters I portrayed the divine process of creation as a two-part process — making mistakes in the status quo and determining which mistakes continue — in a dance of cosmos, life, and human interactions. Similarly, here I am suggesting that the continual disturbances occurring in our world open up new possibilities for living. When the unpredictable Spirit blows where it wills, we are invited to explore new directions that our lives can take. These might be new directions in a particular hour, day, or lifetime. The divine is continually present churning up the waters of life. If we are in tune with the second aspect of divine dynamics, with the Word that signifies the hidden structures of life's possibilities, we will discover new stable patterns — new ways of acting, thinking, and feeling. These will add to the richness of our lives in a continually evolving world.

✐ Chapter 9 ✐

Our Natural Family

I'm trying to change my mind about the way I look at the natural world and its creatures. I'm trying to look at the earth the way Native Americans saw it — Mother Earth. I'm trying to see even insects as "people" — the way the Hopi talk about some of their ancestors in one of their creation stories. It's not easy to do this when I find a wasp in my basement or when a cockroach scurries away from the light I've just turned on as I enter a room. Yet, I think it's important for all of us to see ourselves interconnected with other creatures and the earth — as members of the same natural family.

One reason it's important is to help resolve the problem raised in chapter 3, that of moral motivation in a global village that includes the entire earth and all its inhabitants. Many have recognized that we often know what is right but we don't do it. Paul in the Christian New Testament says, "I do not understand my own actions. For I do not do what I want, but I do the very thing I hate."[1] Today it is even more difficult to do right in our dealings with the natural world. Our scientific technology has given us the power to affect the lives of other species and the ecosystems of our planet in ways that are unprecedented. Many scientists are concerned that our burgeoning human population is challenging the carrying capacity of the earth. Others point out that the "population explosion" of automobiles and some other technologies is threatening our atmosphere with greenhouse gases. We are putting future generations of humans and other species in a crisis that we are just beginning to discern. However, even as we are becoming aware of the trouble we may be causing, we find it difficult to change. In some parts of the world, the idea that we should reduce the rate of population growth is still resisted for biological and cultural reasons. In American society we find it difficult to change our life-styles once we have acquired a high material standard of living that makes daily life so convenient.

There are many things that must be done to help us change our ways of living to insure that life and civilization will continue and flourish in a sustainable manner. New energy efficient technologies, many already invented, must to be placed in the market. Producers and consumers need economic incentives to create an environmentally responsible economy. Politicians need to exercise courageous leadership in passing regulations that can guide living in ways that promote our own well-being and that of our planet. New ways of understanding ourselves in our world must be cultivated to help our minds change so that we will live more in harmony with other creatures on our planet.

The last is especially important because, in the end, it's up to us — to each individual person. Our individual decisions make a difference as to whether the future of our planet will be a flourishing future or one of environmental degradation and diminishing quality of life. The importance of each individual in dealing with environmental issues stands in contrast to how we have been able to deal with another major technological threat to our long-term survival — nuclear war. The nuclear arsenal, as terrifying as it is, is under the control of a few individuals — the leadership of a few countries. Because of this, it has been manageable. However, each of us — every individual — is involved in what happens to our environment. Every child we have or do not have affects human population growth. Every hamburger we buy or do not buy ultimately affects how much forest is cut down to provide pasture to produce more beef. Every trip we take by car to buy a quart of milk affects the emission of greenhouse gases. In contrast to the decision making regarding the use of nuclear weapons that is centralized in the minds of a small number of individuals, the decision making that affects environmental sustainability is in the minds of every person on planet Earth. Therefore, new technologies, economic incentives, and political leadership are not enough. They will be effective only to the extent that the minds of average citizens are open to environmentally sound life-styles. To be open to living differently depends on seeing differently. How we see ourselves in relation to the rest of nature is therefore all important.

We need to find the motivation to act not only for our own immediate well-being but also for the long-term well-being of countless other humans, other species, and our planet. However, as pointed out in chapter three, we are not equipped biologically and culturally to do this. There is no reason why biological evolution should have designed us to feel responsible for the long-term well-being of an entire planet. According to people who study the evolution of morality from a scientific perspective, we have biological propensities to look out for ourselves, to help others if we think we will be helped in return (reciprocal altruism) and to act for the benefit of family, even to the point of self-sacrifice (kin altruism).[2]

Reciprocal altruism is based on our ability to calculate that if we harm others, they might harm us in return. If we do good for others, they are more likely to do good in return. Culturally this has evolved into a sense of fairness or justice: do unto others as you would have them do unto you. This is the basis of social contracts, for example, business agreements to provide goods in return for payment. The idea of social contract has been extended to provide a basis for modern democracies in which a political and economic system has evolved so that people can pursue life, liberty, and happiness in ways that contribute to others pursuing their lives, liberty, and happiness.

As helpful as systems of reciprocal altruism are in motivating people to be moral, acting for the good of others as well as for our own good has its limits. It depends on each individual perceiving that he or she will benefit from the good he or she does for others. When one is called to do good for those who can't reciprocate, then the motivational strength of reciprocal altruism wanes. How can one benefit from doing good to future human generations? How can one benefit from doing good to nonhuman creatures such as sea turtles, rare mosses, and plentiful insects? How can one benefit today from doing good for old growth forests, for the Amazon rain forest with its countless species (many unknown), or for the ozone layer? When we move out of the human sphere into the wider spheres of life and nature, reciprocal altruism becomes more tenuous as a source of moral motivation.

Extending biologically based feelings of care for close kin might be more helpful. However, to do this we need to convince ourselves that we are part of a larger natural family. One way religions have helped people extend kin altruism beyond their immediate families is to use biological metaphors that identify individuals with a wider social community.[3] Early Christians developed the metaphor that each follower of Jesus was a member of the "body of Christ," and the ritual of the Eucharist or Communion made participation in the "body" tangible. This helped create a sense of solidarity that cut across gender, national, racial, and economic boundaries. Islam under the leadership of Muhammad was able to unite factious tribes through warfare, and it reinforced this unity with the metaphor that all who are children of Allah are brothers and sisters. All Muslims are family. Confucians developed the notion of filial piety and extended it to relations with the cosmos. Eikeen Kaibara (1630–1714), a Japanese Confucian philosopher, explains it this way:

> All humans may be said to owe their birth to their parents, but a further inquiry into their origins reveals that we come into being because of nature's law of life. Thus all in the world are children born of heaven and earth, and heaven and earth are the great parents of us all.... Moreover, though we are brought up after birth through the care of our own parents and are sustained by the gracious bounty of the ruler, still if we go to the root of the matter, we find that we sustain ourselves using the things produced by nature for food, dress, housing, and implements. Thus, not only do all humans at the outset come into being because of nature's law of life, but from birth till the end of life they are kept in existence by the support of heaven and earth. We humans surpass all other created things in our indebtedness to the ... bounty of nature.[4]

He then goes on to say that just as we should in return support our own parents, we should be responsible for doing what benefits other creatures and the earth that supports us.

Organic metaphors of family may help reorient our ways of thinking and feeling toward others, so that we are more likely to become motivated to care about the impact of our actions on the rest of the natural world. However, organic metaphors are not likely to be effective unless they make rational sense to those who live in a scientific age. In what follows I suggest that the scientific, evolutionary picture of things helps establish factually our kinship with the rest of the natural world. Then I will present a line of thinking that might show how we have a kinship of values with nonhuman nature. If we can support empirically and rationally that we are indeed one natural family in terms of "facts and values," we may be able to expand our feelings of care for our own families so that we will act for the good of our planet and all its inhabitants.

Contributing to a factual understanding of ourselves as part of a natural family is the developing scientific picture of cosmic evolution. In this picture humans, human culture, and human history are seen as arising out of a physical, chemical, and biological matrix of life on Earth. All other species of life have emerged and continue to emerge out of this same matrix. All species are, in Eric Chaisson's words, "children of the universe."[5] We all are a recent development in the transformations of energy-matter that have been taking place since the beginning of the universe fourteen billion years ago. We all contain "star dust" formed when supernovae created the elements heavier than hydrogen and helium. Everything on Earth has come out of the stars.

Biologically we humans are constituted out of aggregations of cells like all other living creatures. We also are a manifestation of a genetic heritage that begins with reptile-like mammals before the extinction of the dinosaurs sixty-six million years ago. Our DNA code has evolved so that we are biological cousins of other higher primates and more distant relatives of everything else. According to the current scientific picture, we all are part of a unified system of evolving life on our planet. As theologian Philip Hefner says, "On the basis of these scientific perspectives, there is no doubt that *Homo sapiens* is nature's creature. How are we related to the rest of nature? We are kin. . . . Our kinship with nature is not a matter of our preference, nor is it an issue that calls for our acquiescence. It simply is."[6] Therefore, when I say that I am trying to change my mind so that I can see the natural world and all its creatures as Native Americans saw it, I am simply trying to come into touch with the way things are. We *are* all children of heaven and earth as Kaibara puts it. Being part of a natural family is scientifically supported with evidence.

We also are related to all other life forms in terms of value. We all have intrinsic value, which means each of us in our natural family is deserving of respect and care. We all have this kind of value based on the following line of reasoning.[7] My premise is, "If it can value, it is intrinsically valuable." By valuing I mean making some kind of selection among alternatives, preferring some object or some course of action to others. Humans engage in this kind of choice making with some degree of conscious reflection. Like many other animals, we also value nonreflectively, discriminating this object from that by immediate feelings of pleasure and pain. Still other animals, plants, and bacteria (and humans at the level of cells in our bodies) engage in valuing, selecting this rather than that biologically and chemically at the molecular level.[8] Even one-celled organisms such as amoebas and paramecia are able to select and hence value what is nourishing and life supporting, and they are able to reject what is not nourishing and what is life threatening. Because all living things are valuing creatures, we are all worthy of being treated as intrinsically valuable. We all are worthy of having our living affirmed.

Humans who can affirm other life forms reflectively or self-consciously have an added responsibility. Because we cognitively know that we are choosing, rather than just selecting and rejecting on the basis of feelings or of molecular compatibility, we can be held responsible. In moral philosophy, when people make choices, knowing they are making choices, they can be praised or blamed. Being morally responsible is a key characteristic of what it means to be human, although there is some evidence that other primates may on occasion also hold one another responsible.[9] We are morally blameworthy if without good reason, or only for individually selfish reasons, we destroy the lives of others. Therefore, when I see a wasp in my basement or a cockroach in my bathroom, I try to "escort" it outside rather than killing it. They are part of my natural family. In their own ways they value their lives even as I value my own. I observe their self-valuing when they try to defend themselves against a possible threat from me. I would do the same if attacked — fight or flee. We all are members of the family of life. We have value kinship as well as factual kinship with all other created beings who have emerged on our planet through its evolutionary processes.

Respecting and caring about individuals because they have intrinsic value goes only so far in motivating me to change my ways of living in response to environmental problems. This is because our most significant problems go far beyond the individual — increased rate of the extinction of species, deforestation, the loss of biodiversity, and global warming. To become morally motivated to respond responsibly to these issues, I need to extend my argument about valuing from individuals to species themselves. I need to affirm the value of what the individuals are embodiments of, namely a genetic heritage that makes a species what it is.

To affirm the intrinsic value of the genetic heritage of any species, we might consider DNA codes as analogous to recipes for cooking or to plans for a computer. Let's ask which would be worse, to spoil a batch of food or lose the recipe, to damage or destroy a computer or to lose the plans for repairing or making computers? I think we would conclude that the recipe or plan is of greater value than an individual or even a large number of products created according to the plan. Similarly, while the destruction of any individual organism involves a loss of what is intrinsically valuable, an even greater loss of value would be the extinction of the genetic code for a species of organism.

This being so, we should be alarmed at the increasing rate of extinction of species of life. Many individuals in a species can be lost only to be replaced by other individuals. However, extinguishing a species means that we are destroying the possibility of that kind of individual continuing in the future. As Holmes Rolston III suggests, when we extinguish a species of organism we become not just killers but "super killers."[10] We become super killers when we eliminate the biological basis of that species' existence — its unique DNA code.

Individuals have intrinsic value because they are valuing organisms. Species have intrinsic value because they are recipes for the individuals. Now I want to suggest that there is something that is more valuable than either individuals or species. This is the value of that which generates the DNA recipes or plans for the great diversity of life on Earth — creative or productive value. In the natural world creative value is found in the interactions going on in ecosystems. According to Rolston, ecosystems have no value as individual entities, and they are not valuable because they are plans or recipes for particular life forms. They are valuable because interaction among species, and between species and nonliving matter and energy, is a creative matrix. This creative matrix gives birth to new forms of genetic codes and hence to new species and their individuals through what is called natural selection.

To see why this creative matrix is even more valuable than individual organisms or species with their DNA codes, let's return to our analogy of recipes and plans. We can ask, which is worse, to lose the recipes or plans or to lose the creators of the recipes or plans? Similarly, which is worse, to lose individuals and species or to diminish that which creates individuals and species? To live our lives in such a way as to produce greenhouse gases, contribute to global warming, increase the rate of species extinctions, and reduce biodiversity is to alter or reduce the earth's creative capacity. This is morally worse than destroying an individual life, worse than extinguishing a particular species. It is interfering with the matrix, the mother of all, the divine creativity present in the interactions of the universe from the very beginning. This is the sacred heart of the evolving universe of which we have been speaking in previous chapters.

The Native Americans, the Confucians, and many other traditional peoples saw a bigger picture that with the help of modern science and moral reasoning we too can begin to see. We are children of heaven and earth, and its other inhabitants are our family. Even as we draw on the resources of the greater life and world around us to fulfill our own lives, we must also respect and care for the rest of nature with which we share our being. Even more important, we must live in gratitude for the universal creativity that has given us life and feeling and mind and culture. We must live in harmony with the sacred presence and be part of its work of ongoing creation.

Chapter 10

Our Social-Ecological Selves

According to Ralph Wendell Burhoe we are "flow patterns."[1] The core of each one of us is a unique pattern generated out of the interactions of cosmos, biology, and culture. While some rightly say we exist *in* a web of life, Burhoe's idea leads each of us to see ourself *as* a web of life. In contrast to what I initially think myself to be, a relatively solid substance called Karl E. Peters sitting at my computer, occupying a particular space at a particular time, Burhoe suggests that my self extends far beyond my present location. At this moment I am an individual woven out of threads of the history of the universe, my species on this planet, and my culture. I am a social-ecological self, what we might call a "big self." So are you. To understand our social-ecological selves, let's look at ourselves in four different ways. We might imagine this as looking through four different windows of a house. Through each window we can see different aspects of the same thing. Following Burhoe, we can call what we experience our phenomenal, cultural, biological, and cosmic aspects of ourselves.

Let's begin with our phenomenal selves. The word "phenomenon" means appearance. It refers to our selves as they initially appear to us. When we try to look at ourselves without a mirror, what do we see? We see our bodies approximately from the chest down. To see more we have to look in a mirror, but even then we don't see all of ourselves physically. Further, when we "look" inward, we can experience ourselves observing, feeling, and thinking. We also have an awareness that we are a subject capable of observing and to some extent directing our attention to feelings, thoughts, and body observations. If we attempt to locate this directing, observing subject — our "I" — it seems to be located in our heads, behind our eyes. But, try as hard as we might, we cannot observe it any more than that.

All this I call our phenomenal self. Our phenomenal self is what we are aware of through everyday sense observation and introspection. It does not last much beyond one hundred years. Some have claimed that the introspected self (the mind as an observing, thinking, and feeling subject) endures beyond the life of the body. It is what many have called the "soul."

However, this concept of a substantive soul, a kind of spiritual substance that is our self-conscious subject existing beyond the grave, is called into question by modern science. This is because of evidence that correlates our observing, thinking, feeling — and our self-consciousness of these activities — with the physical and electrical-chemical states of various systems of our brains. Insofar as this correlation is a strong one, and insofar as there is evidence that at death the physical brain dies and then disintegrates along with the rest of the body, it is difficult to understand how our self-conscious subjectivity can continue in a disembodied, dis-brained way. From a scientific perspective, it seems that both our bodies and our inner subjectivity are not likely to survive beyond our physical life span. Because of this Burhoe suggests that our phenomenal body/mind is not the real core of our human nature. The real core is something that endures beyond the life span of the phenomenal self. Also, it is something that gives rise to the phenomenal self. It is our social-ecological self, our big self.

We can begin to see one strand of our big self, our cultural self, through some everyday observations. I can remember a time when I was very small, even though now I am relatively large. I also can remember a time when I did not know much or understand much. I now observe younger people and children today in the same condition. Along with my body, my mind also has grown.

A key to the growth of our minds is language. Beginning when we were very young, language entered our brains through our ears. Not only did we hear single words, but we heard patterns of words. As a result our physical brains, all the time being nourished with food, are also nurtured with the grammar and syntax, as well as the vocabulary, of our "native" tongues. We now know that people who use languages with different grammars and syntaxes think differently in some ways. So these aspects of language play a role in how we think; they help shape our minds. In effect, the language of a particular society is a recipe for the human minds in that society, a recipe encoded into the physical brains of children as they grow up. This recipe is what Burhoe calls the "culturetype," what I am calling our cultural selves.

Along with ways of thinking embedded in language, a culturetype includes ways of doing things: ways of gathering, growing, processing, and eating food; ways of building houses and other structures of human habitation; ways of getting around with transportation; ways of playing; ways of being religious. Underlying all of these ways of doing things, manifested in them, and programmed into the brain through them, is a society's value system. At the heart of the cultural recipe lie the values, goals, and purposes that shape our actions. The culturetype shapes both my thinking and acting. It even shapes my feelings. By doing this it gives rise to much of my character and personality.

Culture is not the only thing that shapes our character and personality. Our biology — governed by another recipe, our genetic code — also plays a major role in how our phenomenal selves are woven. To "see" this clearly, we need to move beyond our own common sense observation and introspection, supplementing and refining it with the observations and theories of contemporary genetics, sociobiology, and biological anthropology. If we take this information and digest it, we can begin to create a story about how we came to be what we are.

We began as a zygote, a union of the DNA or genetic material from our two parents. Our DNA code is equivalent to an encyclopedia of information that is "read out" as the cells of the zygote multiply in various environments. The nature of the environments are critical for the DNA recipe's expression. Equally critical is the arrangement of molecules of the DNA recipe itself.

One the one hand, if we are growing inside our mother's womb and do not get the proper nourishment through the placenta, or if our mother is an alcoholic or drug addict, we will be born with serous brain defects. These affect our ability to acquire the language and other features of our society's culturetype, and thus the development not only of our bodies but also of our minds, or how we observe and feel, think and act. Likewise, as we leave the womb other environments come into play. Because our brains are not fully developed when we are born, nutrition in the first six months is critical. Even after our brains are fully developed and healthy, nutrition still can affect our mental functioning. On the other hand, the DNA code itself may be "defective" for any number of reasons. The code may give us tendencies for poor eyesight, diabetes, schizophrenia, or any one of thousands of recognized genetically based disorders. These too will be factors in the development of our bodies and minds — and our resulting observing, feeling, acting, and thinking.

These considerations illustrate that our phenomenal selves are woven out of the threads of biology and culture; we are the result of genotypes interacting with various environments to develop our biological structures and functioning, and of "culturetypes" that through sense experience nourish our brains with language, behaviors, and values that shape our observing, feeling, thinking, and acting. As Philip Hefner says, our species "*Homo sapiens* is itself a nodal point wherein two streams of information come together and coexist. The one stream is inherited genetic information, the other is cultural information. Both of these streams come together in the central nervous system" — in our brains.[2] Together they shape our selves.

There is still a third strand or stream of what we are — beyond culturetype and genotype — without which we would not be born and would not continue to exist. Looking through still another window we can see our cosmic self. Atoms and molecules, organized via amino acids as proteins, provide the material for our biological selves. This material in turn is organized according to our genetic recipes, which also are created out of atoms and molecules, organized via nucleic acids, sugars, and phosphates into deoxyribonucleic acid, DNA.

Along with the atoms and molecules that are the basic material for us, we are constituted also by the laws of nature, the universe's information system. These laws organize energy-matter at the atomic and molecular level. They govern such phenomena as the formation and functioning of stars, the relations between Earth and the Moon that affect the tides, and all kinds of physical and chemical workings on our planet. Present throughout the universe, laws of gravity, electromagnetism, atomic interactions, and chemistry are also present in us. They provide a kind of cosmic recipe or "cosmotype" for the functioning of all things including ourselves at the atomic and molecular levels. Nature is in us as much as we are in nature. We are woven webs of cosmos as well as of bios, as well as of culture.

As an example of how important our cosmic self is, let us look at our dependence on the Sun. We all know that the Sun is the primary energy source that makes all life possible on our planet, just as plants and animals are the food source that makes human biological living possible. What is now becoming known is that our subjective, mental states can be affected by the amount of sunlight we receive. There is scientific evidence that some people are subject to depression if they do not receive enough light — some more than others. When days grow shorter, some people manifest what is called "seasonal affective disorder" — SAD. Earth's cycling around the Sun can affect how we feel. We are part of a total earth-sun system.

All this analysis indicates that we are webs of reality, woven out of the threads of culture, biology, and cosmos according to recipes (structures of language and values, DNA codes, and laws of nature) in each. As webs of reality each of us is a manifestation of the evolving universe. Furthermore, as webs of reality each of us in various ways survives the death of our phenomenal selves.

Because our phenomenal selves, including our subjective experience of ourselves, are woven out of culture, biology, and cosmos, when the strands that make up what we are dissipate, our phenomenal selves die. When our physical, chemical, biological bodies cease to function, the web of our lives unravels. Our phenomenal selves do not last much more than a hundred years. However, as we live here and now, we weave new threads that become our contributions to culture, biology, and cosmos. We continue through our other selves. If we now ask how long our other selves exist, we can see that we are in fact much older and have a much longer future that we might at first suspect.

If we consider how long our culture has existed, we realize that each of us is as old as our language and the value system that shapes our living and acting. We are from five hundred to three thousand years old. If we reflect on how long our DNA recipes and other features of human biology have existed, then we are millions of years old. If we ask how long our cosmic self has existed, then we must answer that we are as old as the universe itself. According to the first law of thermodynamics, energy-matter is neither created nor destroyed. It is only transformed from one pattern into another. Therefore, we contain in us — in all of our selves — after many cosmic, biological, and cultural transformations the energy that was present at the origin of the universe. The universe evolved according to its fundamental laws into hydrogen, helium, galaxies, and stars. It further evolved into heavier atoms resulting from massive exploding stars, planetary systems, and the earth filled with life. Many of these various transformations of energy-matter have become a part of each one of us. In our own bodies, we represent a history of the universe.

How old then are we? Phenomenally a few decades, culturally a few centuries or millennia, biologically millions of years, cosmically fourteen billion years. How long will we continue? Phenomenally a few more years, culturally probably a few more centuries or millennia, biologically millions of years or (if we do not destroy ourselves first) perhaps until our Sun dies five billion years from now, and cosmically until the universe ends, which may be never. It all depends on how we think of our selves. In Burhoe's thinking, the real core of our human nature is what endures beyond the grave of our phenomenal bodies and minds. Our particular web of reality, woven out of cultural, biological, and cosmic threads, contributes back more cultural, biological, and cosmic threads — out of which other phenomenal selves can be woven. We may not have a self-conscious phenomenal immortality, a substantive soul. That is an older understanding of what we are and how we might continue. But we have something just as significant if we do not make our atomized egos the be-all and end-all of everything. We have a social-ecological-evolutionary kind of immortality as part of the fabric of an evolving universe. Seen as a web of cosmos, life, and culture, we are really big, big selves.

❧ Chapter 11 ❧

Morality and Meaning for Our "Big Selves"

In describing what it means to have a big self, I have suggested that we have a special kind of immortality — a social-ecological-evolutionary kind of immortality. This idea offers us an important implication for morality and meaning: what matters is not just how long we live but how well we live in the sense of contributing further to human culture, biological well-being, and the ecosystems of the earth. This is the primary responsibility of our phenomenal self. The phenomenal self is not as long-lived as our other selves. However, it is a critical weaving together of strands from culture, biology, and cosmos; and it is the means through which the other selves are reproduced and continue into the future. It also is the means by which our other selves can be self-consciously modified, so that the cultural-biological-cosmic "souls" of each of us — which come together to form us as we are now — can be changed for better or worse in light of how we live and die.

In speaking of the phenomenal self and its importance in relation to eternity (primarily in cultural terms), Max Rudolf Lemberg writes:

I believe that eternity does not begin after my death; it was before I came and will remain when I die. But above all it is during my life here on earth, and this is indeed the only time during which I am responsible for my contribution to it.... It is, I believe, untrue that what I have done during my life, however insignificant in itself, will not count from the viewpoint of eternity. What I mean is not that it will be remembered. Nobody remembers the man who split the first flint or lit the first fire.... Nobody remembers the first

74

woman who spun or planted seeds. My individual unity may be remembered for a few years and that of the great man, Jesus, for thousands of years. It is not important whether my name or any special deed of mine will be remembered; it will certainly not be remembered forever. However, what I have done, whatever it was, good or evil, has become eternal in the sense that it has become an indestructible irremovable part and parcel of the tissue of life of mankind.... Not only books or discoveries or statements but even passing acts of generosity or lack of it — anything which has influenced other persons, adult or child, belongs to the eternal realm, even a mere loving act, thought, or gesture. That I shall not survive my uniqueness of person may be a serious blow to my self-love, but the contributions of myself and millions of other persons are not in vain.... [1]

When I read this passage I think of a man who was crippled from birth with something like cerebral palsy. He crawled around his home, pushed himself in a wagon around his small town, and talked in a guttural stammer that was barely understandable. He lived with his mother for most of his life; after she died he spent the rest of his years in a nursing home. He died when he was sixty-six. Yet, the funeral home was packed for his burial service. The minister spoke on the parable of the talents from the Christian Gospel of Matthew.[2] This parable is about people who use their gifts wisely. As I sat in the front row of the funeral chapel, I wondered how the minister was going to apply this to my Uncle Arthur. Dependent on others during all the narrow circle of his life, what did he have to offer? The minister said Arthur Peters had one talent: he always made people feel welcome. As I heard this I thought of how he always greeted people who came to see him. He would offer a palsied handshake, a crooked smile, and slurred "Hewo, howareyou?" It was "a mere loving act, thought, or gesture" — consistently done. Lemberg suggests that in such ways our phenomenal self can contribute to eternity perhaps as much as some great discoveries.

Even though its span of time is relatively brief, the phenomenal self plays an essential role in reproducing and transforming the flow patterns that make up our "soul." It continues to spin the threads out of which it was created, and it can spin new threads that are then rewoven into other phenomenal selves. This gives to each of us right now — in our daily living — considerable responsibility for our own future beyond the death of our bodies — the future of our other selves in relation to the larger culture, life, and cosmos in which we live. Martin Luther King, referring I think to his phenomenal self, once said that it is not how long we live that is important but the quality of our lives. The same holds true of our other selves. It is not the fact that we will continue for hundreds, thousands, millions, and billions of years that is most significant; it is *how* we will continue that matters.

How we continue as "big selves" enlarges our sense of morality. What we take as significant moral issues must include not only what is important to individuals. In a communal concept of self, significant moral issues must also include what is good for our society, environment, and cosmos, because that is how each of us continues to live beyond the grave.

For example, and here each of us must answer for his or her cultural self, do we want to live the kind of life that enhances or diminishes culture? Do we want to support so-called higher forms of art or trivializations of human artistic potential? Do we want to support love, friendship, and sympathy or aggression, dehumanization, and hatred? Do we want to work for a just, peaceful, and ecologically sustainable planet or do we want to support those human enterprises that feed on greed, racism, sexism, warfare, and environmental degradation? In short, we cannot avoid having an impact on the lives of others, especially on future generations. As Lemberg says, there is no doubt that through our influence on others each of us will survive, weaving more threads of human culture. But the kinds of threads we weave will make a difference in how we continue in the lives of others.

The same is true of our biology. As we become more aware of how our actions affect our environment and how the environment in turn affects the development of future generations, we must recognize our responsibility to the biological future of humanity. Most already recognize responsibility to their phenomenal offspring —

their immediate children. When they do not, others in society recognize the "rights" of children and pass laws against such behavior
as child abuse. However, if the genes transmitted to the future are
a part of our core nature, our "souls," do we not also have a similar responsibility to protect the expression of those genes in future
humans? Human reproduction can be affected by the quality of the
physical-chemical world that shapes what we are. Chemical and nuclear pollution, as well as ozone layer depletion, which increases the
amount of ultraviolet radiation from the Sun, can alter the physical
capabilities of future generations. Our actions that affect our environment can alter the biological threads out of which humans are
woven. Child abuse is not something we only can do to our own
children. Environmental degradation can in effect abuse children
of future generations.

Further, when our phenomenal selves die, what do we do with
our organs, cells, molecules, and atoms that make up our biological
and cosmic selves? Here too we can perhaps enhance the quality
of lives of others, not just humans but other living organisms on
our planet. Perhaps we can donate healthy organs to preserve the
lives of other individuals. We also can think about how to dispose
of the remainder of our bodies so that our molecules and atoms can
be used to weave further threads of cosmos, life, and even culture.
Recently we have become concerned with recycling products we
have used. Can we also think about recycling our own bodies? If we
are embedded within nature and nature is in us, we might want to
consider our own organic impact for better or worse on the rest of
the planet.

In my environmental ethics course, when we discuss human self-
understanding in light of ideas like the big self and social, ecological
immortality, I ask my students about environmentally good ways
to recycle our bodies when we die. They usually respond, "Bury
me in a pine box and plant a tree over me; I'll decompose and
nourish the tree; my atoms will become part of the tree." Others
say, "Simply put me out sight, out doors, and let the birds and other
creatures eat me; let me be a resource for nourishing other living
beings." These ideas may startle us at first, because we have been
culturally programmed to think differently about death. Through

custom and regulations our culture instructs us to try to preserve our phenomenal bodies as long as possible in hermetically sealed caskets. However, if we really value our cosmic selves, including the proteins, carbohydrates, vitamins, and minerals that make us what we are, might we not want our bodies to decay and nourish other forms of life? In this manner we could make a small contribution to the well-being of the planet even in death.

As we begin to see some of the moral significance of having social-ecological selves, we might ask, "What kinds of general guidelines should we follow so that our big selves in their various aspects can continue?" In terms of evolutionary theory, two general things are required for the continuation of our selves. On the one hand, we must live within certain boundaries set by the laws of cosmos, biology, and culture. On the other hand, we must be able to create, to spin alternative ways of living in order to be adaptive in a continually changing world. In other words we must be free. Freedom is not a luxury. In a world that is constantly changing, the freedom to explore new possibilities for living is a necessity.

These two conditions are necessary for the continuation not only of humans but of all living things: they can be characterized as law and freedom; tradition and innovation; natural selection and random variation; and necessity and chance. However labeled, together they constitute fundamental requirements for continuation. These requirements for continuing to live are embedded in a more comprehensive picture of the universe. The universe evolves through all its stages as a result of fluctuations disturbing the status quo and of laws according to which some fluctuations reach new stable states — what I suggest is the divine spirit and word in the dance of creation. There is thus a permissiveness in nature, supporting new explorations, as well as a lawfulness that controls how much exploring can be done. In Christian theological terms, nature exhibits grace and judgment. Because each of us is embedded in nature, our living is granted grace and freedom to explore but is also subject to judgment and the boundaries of law. Let me illustrate in terms of culture, biology, and cosmos.

In his book on world religions, Huston Smith points out how a society following the Jewish Ten Commandments can be both permissive and lawful. The commandments are "wise restraints that make men free."[3] Taking, for example, "Thou shalt not kill," Smith asks us to consider all that we can do to our fellow human beings. We can do all kinds of things to them for good or ill. One thing we should not do, however, is kill them. The same is true of most of the other commandments as well. Permissiveness within law is possible when commandments regulating human social relations are formulated in the negative: "Thou shalt not." While sometimes criticized, the negative formulation actually permits great freedom in human behavior, even as it sets certain boundaries beyond which the behavior should not go. A society with clear moral and legal boundaries formulated as negative laws can also allow for the kind of creative freedom necessary for the members of that society to respond to changing circumstances. Negative judgment comes into play only when the boundaries are tested, as indeed they can be. When this occurs, however, those who challenge the boundaries must be willing to pay the price of "civil disobedience" or the costs of social revolution.

The same kind of lawfulness combined with permissiveness is present in our biology. Think of all the things we can do with our bodies and brains — all the different things we can experience and the different ways we can think and act. However, there also are certain biological boundaries. We cannot violate the necessities of nutrition and expect to remain healthy. We cannot jump from tall buildings in violation of the law of gravity without paying the price of freedom extended too far. In some cases individuals may have to live within special constraints because of how their DNA has interacted with specific environments to shape the functioning of their bodies. I remember a student who had manic-depressive or bipolar disorder. An exceptionally bright person, he could not fully accept the fact that he was dependent on lithium to moderate his excessive mood swings. For him the taking of lithium was a requirement he had to acknowledge, a boundary he could not ignore. When he met this requirement, he had considerable freedom to think and do what he wanted in his life. However, when he tried to free himself from the requirement of taking lithium, he paid the price and wound up in the psychiatric ward of the local hospital.

Similarly, for species of living organisms, a kind of freedom is present in the exploration of various genetic combinations, experimenting with the genotype through random variation, giving rise to diversity among the individuals of a particular species. Yet, all individuals must meet certain requirements to continue: they must feed themselves; defend themselves against life-threatening predators, including microorganisms that cause disease; and reproduce themselves. Any changes in the genotype that hinder individuals in a species from living long enough to reproduce themselves are selected against, negatively judged. This is the key to natural selection.

Sometimes for living organisms, something as simple as size sets a boundary. Invertebrates, for example, cannot get too large, or they will collapse under their own weight. Biologist Guenter Stent once pointed this out when he discussed some horror movies about monster spiders. Even though they are frightful products of human imagination and special effects engineering, Stent argued that in reality monster spiders could never exist. According to Newton's laws of gravitation, because it has no inner skeletal structure, any such organism would collapse under its own weight and die before it could damage anything else.

Further, one can observe the same two conditions operating in the physical-chemical or inanimate world. A wide variety of combinations of atoms and molecules, with their resulting structures and functions, are possible — as long as they satisfy the basic requirements of physical and chemical laws.

As individual webs of culture, biology, and cosmos, these same two conditions apply to us during our lifetime as phenomenal selves. We are granted freedom to make innovations in how we live as cultural, biological, and physical-chemical creatures. Some of our explorations may even challenge the boundaries, the limits beyond which we cannot go. At times our conception of what the boundaries are may be false; we may have more leeway than once thought. However, sooner or later, we will come up against some boundaries. Attempting to go beyond them will result in our individual degeneration and death, the impoverishment or death of a society, or even the diminishment or death of our species. We will have transgressed the fundamental requirements that make the universe, including us, what it is. However, freedom also is a fundamental requirement, necessary in an ever changing world. Not to explore by chance or with intention is again to risk being subject to negative judgment.

Combining these two fundamental requirements — permissiveness and freedom on the one hand, and cultural, biological, and cosmic laws on the other — is a good way to understand what it means to be related to the divine creativity in our midst. Creativity is the process that constantly gives rise to new possibilities for being and then selects from those possibilities what continues to exist. This twofold dance of becoming is the foundation of cosmos, of life, of society, and of our big selves.

As we become related to the divine process of creation in our midst, participating in it, our lives become meaningful. Our living is in harmony with the larger scheme of things. Our phenomenal selves find meaning here and now when we continue the past and when we build on the past in creative freedom, when within the boundaries established by the laws of nature and culture we experiment and explore to help produce the remarkable diversity of life and thought.

Sometimes our exploring may test the boundaries and perhaps even change them. Some laws of physics, chemistry, biology, and society are very stable and inviolable. It is difficult to imagine overturning the law of gravity, or doing without food and energy, or not transmitting language and values to the next generation. However, one can imagine altering other requirements that are not so fundamental. In a changing world, which values should and should not be transmitted to the next generation remains a question that can be freely explored. Even though all societies require the transmission of some set of values, the content of that set may change.

Many today find meaning for their lives in challenging values related to a hierarchical understanding of nature and human society, in which humans are superior to all other creatures and men are superior to women. Environmentalist and liberation movements are to be regarded as innovations in human cultural evolution that test the current boundary conditions embodied in codes of law, morality, and custom in many societies. These new movements are experiments that will help destabilize existing social structures in the hope that new and better social systems will be created.

If we look at biological organisms, we see that through random, genetic variation, they are always experimenting, testing the boundaries, attempting to find new ways of living in a changing world. In highly stable environments, new variations are likely to fail. They are not reproduced. However, when the environment is rapidly changing, new variations may be important for survival. They may help continue the species as its modifies itself to adapt to new circumstances.

The same holds true of human societies. Part of the purpose of living is to engage in experimenting with new patterns of living. When a society is cohesive and is well adapted to its larger biological and physical environment, individual and small group experimentation is not likely to be successful. Even in periods of rapid change experimentation is still risky; however, it also is essential for the long-term viability of the society.

The point of all this is that when we explore the boundaries as well as live within their limits, we are part of an evolving universe — a total system of reality that has given rise to both the permissiveness of living and the constraints on the permissiveness. The creative process, which is the sacred center of this evolving universe, continually brings new things into being even as it continues some traditional ways of living. This process is what we have understood as divine. Living within long-established requirements of nature and culture is living according to the "will of God." Exploring the boundaries — even at risk — is also living in harmony with the Holy.

❧ Chapter 12 ❧

The Development of the Earth and the Quality of Life

When I think about living in our natural family, aware that we are big selves, and trying to live in harmony with divine creativity, I feel morally responsibility for how I live. Once I recognize my kinship with all of life, I realize my human responsibility to care for other members of our natural family. Once I see how our big selves continue on in culture, biosphere, and cosmos, I feel responsible for how I continue. Once I see my own creating and conserving as part of an ongoing creativity that is the source of being and value, and in relation to which our lives can be meaningful, I want to discover ways to fulfill myself that also allow other creatures to fulfill themselves.

One kind of fulfillment, the materialistic development of the earth for human ends, is helping place our global village in peril. For the past few hundred years some human beings have been developing the earth. First Europeans and Americans, now joined by people on the Pacific Rim and elsewhere, have been using the insights of science and the tools of technology to engineer a better life, defined as a higher material standard of living. As they have done this, they have diminished resources, exploited people, and have made their own lives more stressful. As Robert Heilbroner points out in his book *An Inquiry into the Human Prospect*, the so-called better life in affluent societies has not increased happiness.[1]

We need to seek another kind of fulfillment, one that is consistent with the Taoist notion of a divine dance that goes nowhere in particular but yet brings great joy and satisfaction in a fullness of living. Instead of talking about fulfillment, we might talk about "fill-fullment," living richly in the present moment.

Another way of thinking about living fully in the present is to talk about the quality of our lives. Even with this, however, we must beware of the danger of living here and now, attaining lives high in quality for ourselves at the expense of other people and the wider natural world. How can we live and flourish without impoverishing others? How can we be filled full without emptying the cup of life's possibilities for others? How can we have lives of high quality while at the same time allowing the planet to continue to sustain human civilization and all its other inhabitants? What kind of quality of life can we have?

Before I offer a definition of quality of life it will be helpful to ask what is life? What does it mean to live? I suggest that to live means not only to exist but to exist in a good state of physical and mental health. Even when we are not in full health, we often can live long enough to reproduce, and thereby satisfy the conditions of evolution for survival. However, individuals who are healthy and able to develop their physical, intellectual, and other personal capabilities are more likely to function successfully in society and be more effective in both reproducing themselves biologically and in transmitting culturally their patterns of living.

At the level of basic physical and mental health, some ways in which people are developing the earth give cause for concern. When long-lasting pesticides get into food chains, onto dinner tables, and into the milk of mothers, they affect the development of healthy human beings. When water is contaminated by industrial pollutants, or if there is simply not enough good water available in a heavily populated area, people's physical health is affected. When people work in a chemical plant in Hopewell, Virginia, or in the coal mines of Europe, or breath smog from automobile exhausts in Mexico City or Seoul, Korea, their health is affected. We should be concerned about local, regional, and global pollution when it affects the physical and mental well-being of people. Without physical and mental health, quality of life becomes more difficult if not impossible.

To develop and keep our physical and mental health we engage in maintenance activities. We seek food, shelter, clothing, and relaxation. We have children so that life may continue in future generations. In agricultural societies, maintenance activities are most often done in direct relation to the earth. In industrialized and urbanized societies, we are further removed from the direct means of physical self-maintenance and rely on making money to obtain what we need to nourish, shelter, and enjoy ourselves. For more and more people in our developing global village, earning money is critical to developing and maintaining physical and mental health.

Here we sometimes find a conflict between protecting the environment and using industrial technology. In many situations where industry is harming the environment, often with resulting harm to human beings, the elimination or redesigning of those industries results in layoffs of workers. Without work they are unable to maintain their basic well-being, their physical and mental health, with the further result that their quality of life is also diminished. Of course, the real solution is to provide employment in industries that will not adversely affect the natural world and the health of the employed and others living nearby. The point here, however, is that economics cannot be ignored. Personal income is a necessary condition in many societies today for maintaining physical and mental health.

If physical and mental health are maintained, then it is more likely that one can live a life of quality. Quality of life can be defined as what we have when we expand the breadth and depth of experience and achievement. Expanding the breadth of our experience means increasing the variety of experiences we can have within the boundaries set by the moral codes of societies. This variety may take many forms. One example is having contact with people from diverse cultures and coming to understand and appreciate their ways of living. Science and technology, in bringing about the global village, are giving more people an opportunity to expand their quality of life through travel to other countries, educational programs on television, books and magazines, and web sites on the Internet. The opportunity to expand the breadth of experience is more available to more people today than ever before in history. It is one of the beneficial products of the development of the earth's resources by science and technology.

Even as we seek to increase variety, we can also try to experience our world in greater depth — delving into one aspect of experience to gain as much from it as possible. For example, scientists with the aid of more and more sophisticated technology can probe deeper into a cell or atom. By doing this they discover "worlds" just as exciting as those discovered by travelers to other countries. For scientists, the technology that produces such instruments as electron microscopes and radio telescopes improves the quality of their lives. Yet, we should not forget that the depth of experience does not always require the kind of technology that uses material resources. In its original meaning of *techne*, technology can also be the art of doing something. Ancient religions have developed sophisticated techniques for exploring various states of human consciousness. Through "technologies" of meditation, a Buddhist monk may realize a depth of experience as enlightening as the understanding achieved by a modern scientist. On a more everyday level, partners in marriage or friends who have developed the art of conversation may also achieve a depth of experience in relationship that is qualitatively rich.

In seeking breadth and depth of experience of ourselves, other human beings, and the physical world, we are living primarily in a receptive mode. Although we engage in activities that put us in touch with what we are experiencing, we are still on the receiving end. I suggest that part of having a life high in quality also involves developing an active side of ourselves. We may develop new physical or intellectual skills such as swimming, bike riding, playing basketball, skiing, writing poetry, programming computers, taking photographs, and playing a saxophone. We may also develop relational capabilities such as empathy, compassion, and empowering the development of others. We may develop some of these to the highest level of which we are capable. By developing our skills we are able to create — to achieve something in our lives that continues on in the minds and lives of others as a strand of our cultural selves — giving us one form of "objective immortality." Scientists create hypotheses in the hopes they will be verified and become accepted theory. Artists create sculptures and compose music. Therapists develop and apply insights in human relationships. Educators develop teaching skills and construct curricula. Scholars write papers and books. By seeking breadth and depth of experience and variety and excellence of achievement, we humans not only live; we acquire quality in our lives.

Earlier I indicated that before we can have quality of life, we need some degree of physical and mental health. The healthier we are, the more we are able to experience and accomplish. Being able to satisfy the basic needs of human existence makes it easier to expand the breadth and depth of our experience, and to develop skills and create. One other thing is helpful — meeting basic needs with a minimum expenditure of energy over the shortest range of time. The less time and effort we spend on maintenance activities, the more time and energy we have to experience our world and create. Conversely, the more time and effort we have to put into maintaining our basic well-being, the less time and energy we have for gaining quality in our lives.

This brings me to the main point I wish to make in this chapter. The development of the earth through science, technology, and industrialization has created a situation in which most of us in developed countries have to spend less time on maintenance activities that did our ancestors. This has given more of us more time to travel, read, further our education, engage in sports, think about scientific problems, meditate, and create works of art than in earlier societies. However, at the same time, our scientific, technological, and industrial development of the earth has reached a point where we are diminishing the quality of life and the health of other humans, destroying the lives of individual natural creatures, and extinguishing entire species in our natural family. We also may be reaching a point where the quality of our own lives may actually become diminished, because we once again are having to spend more time and energy maintaining our health and meeting our basic needs. Even as we seek quality of life, some of our own activities can turn back on us and diminish that quality.

Some of what I've already written hints at this, but let me explain further. Although activities that support life maintenance can be distinguished from those that contribute to the quality of life, often the same activities do both. Scientists, artists, philosophers, and educators can both create and get paid for what they do. Thus they maintain themselves with work that also brings quality of life. Others can do this as well. Carpenters, bricklayers, contractors — and even the heads of large land development corporations — can derive satisfaction from creative activity. Developing the earth is achieving. It is creative. Those doing it gain some quality of life.

This point about the creative activity of builders was brought home to me when I rented an apartment from an old retired gentleman. This man, an immigrant from Sweden, told me how pleased he was about what he had accomplished during his lifetime. As a young man he had been a construction worker on the railroads, and he was proud that he had helped to build something that was of benefit to others. He was even more satisfied that he had been a contractor. The pleasure he took in pointing out to me houses he had built forty years earlier, which were still being lived in, was an indication that he had done more than just exist. He had created something. His life had quality. Perhaps it is this way with many who are materialistically developing the earth. They earn a living for their own self-maintenance and that of their families, but they also are realizing fulfillment.

However, the creative achievements of such builders can lead to a situation that restricts the quality of life for others, a situation in which people have to spend more time and effort in personal maintenance and have less personal energy for breadth and depth of experience and achievement. When I was a boy, I listened to my grandmother describe how as a child she used to walk five miles through the woods to school. When I became a working adult, I made a similar five-mile trip to Rollins College — a place where I earned a living, expanded my experience through learning with my students, created classroom teaching activities, and wrote articles for publication. While it took my grandmother about one hour and fifteen minutes to walk to school, I drove the five miles in fifteen minutes, thanks to the creativity of many in the automobile industry and some road builders. Compared to my grandmother, I saved one full hour each way — two hours a day round trip — on what was essentially a maintenance activity of transporting myself to and from my place of work. I was able to use the time saved to increase the quality of my life.

However, the development of the land in central Florida continues — more people, more homes, more cars. Even with the expansion of the roads to six-lane speedways, on some days because of the "weekly accident," it again took one hour and fifteen minutes to get to school. That was how long it took when I lived in New Jersey and commuted to Manhattan. What then did I really gain compared with my grandmother? I spent the same time in a maintenance activity as she did a over a century ago, and I was caught in the stop and start driving of a long chain of energy consuming, air polluting motor vehicles, hazardous to my health and hard on my nerves. My grandmother, in her five-mile walk to school, at least enjoyed the West Virginia brooks and woods and, probably, the creativity of her imagination. The development of the earth does not always improve the quality of life.

Another line of thinking that brings me to the same conclusion begins with asking: "Quality of life for whom?" At the local level this question arises, for example, when land developers build on flood plains. They create and with the income they earn they maintain themselves. However, the buyers of homes in such developments may find that their maintenance activities increase if heavy rains bring about flooding and they have to spend more time coping with high water. The question "Quality of life for whom?" also arises on a much larger scale. Our society as a whole, with its sophisticated technologies and industrial institutions, is rapidly using up resources from around the world in the creation of a life-style that has more opportunities for expanding experience and achievement than anyone else has known. At the same time, there are many people in countries that supply our resources who do not have much quality of life and who are suffering from poor physical and mental health. Many do not have life as I have defined it, much less quality of life. Finally, the question "Quality of life for whom?" arises when we look to the future. What right do we have today to develop the earth in such a way as to destroy the lives of countless species, impoverish the creativity of ecosystems, and create conditions such that future generations will find it difficult to have the quality of life we have?

We also can ask: "Do *we* really have a high quality of life?" Does all this development give us greater breadth and depth of experience and achievement? Not always. I have discovered this in my own life. For years my wife and I were fortunate enough to live on a lake. Like many others we invested some of our extra money in a speed boat, which we used to show visitors the lake and to water ski. Speed boats are relatively new inventions. Our neighbor had a much older mode of water transportation, a canoe. One evening he gave us permission to take his canoe for a sunset ride. Our sixty-five acre lake was entirely calm. No one else was on the water. As we canoed silently along the shore, we enjoyed the sounds of the evening, the sunset, and the quiet conversation between ourselves. I was amazed at all the things I saw and heard that I had never seen and heard before — certainly never in my speed boat. I began to wonder, how useful is a speed boat in achieving quality of life? Certainly, it enabled me to develop skills associated with water skiing. At thirty miles per hour I experienced the wind rushing by and the noise of the motor. And if we had boated on a river it might have taken us somewhere and expanded our experience. However, I began to realize that, if one is seeking a wide variety and depth of experience close to home, perhaps the canoe brings more quality into one's life than a speed boat. Perhaps the quality of life doesn't always depend on the most recent science, technology, and industry. Perhaps the development of the earth, as we have been doing it for the past few hundred years with a costly expenditure of materials and energy, is not the only — not the best — way to achieve a life of high quality.

In part, a life of high quality depends on the kinds of experiences we seek to increase the breadth and depth of our experience. It depends on the kinds of activities we engage in to increase the breadth and depth of our achievement. Experience and achievement can be related to the different kinds of good we seek. According to Daniel R. DeNicola, there are three kinds of such good.[2] One kind is gained at the expense of others. Either it is in limited supply or acquiring it hinders other people's ability to acquire it. Material things are such goods. If we seek a high quality of life that depends on consuming large amounts of energy and matter, we compete with other humans and other creatures for the limited resources of the earth.

A second kind of good is gained without hindering others from also attaining it. Examples are experiencing the warmth of sunshine, the glow of sunsets, the colors of flowers, the activities of birds and animals, invigorating walks, and pleasant conversations with people we meet in passing. There are many simple gifts that nature and human interaction give us that all can enjoy.

Finally, there is a kind of good that is actually creative. The more people seek it, the more of it there is. Developing our capacities for friendship and love creates opportunities for others to be our friends and to love us in return. Seeking peace among the variety of the world's peoples increases peace for everyone. We might call this kind of good spiritual good, because if we seek quality of life through love and peace, we use a modest amount of energy and matter and we give off no material pollution as we increase breadth and depth of experience and achievement for ourselves and others.

It seeking this "spiritual" kind of good we live our lives in harmony with our natural family. We also fulfill our big selves, weaving positive strands of character into the future in such a way that others are not hindered from doing the same. The quality of our lives does not require developing the earth in ways that diminish it in the long run. We can gain what we seek as human beings by being responsible social-ecological selves.

Chapter 13

Seeking Our Sacred Center

Basic life questions are answered not only intellectually. They are answered with our whole being, with the way we live our lives. When I was younger, one question I sought to answer was, "What good do I want to accomplish?" How can I have the best life possible? Gradually I have come to realize that my quality of life is enhanced more by nonmaterial than by material goods. Yes, I feel it is good for me to have a nice house, furnishings, clothes, car, books, and a computer. But without a loving family and friends these things don't mean much. Material goods do not satisfy my basic longings the way that spiritual goods do.

Today, another basic question I am trying to answer in my living is, "What kind of person do I want to be?" Reflecting on this question, I find I want to be friendly, loving, caring, compassionate, curious, open to new possibilities, intelligent, and, insofar as is possible, wise. What has become good for me is not so much what I can acquire. It has become what I can be.

However, even though I want to be this way, I also find that I sometimes feel angry, resentful, and jealous. Sometimes I behave in ways that could bring harm to other human beings and other forms of life. I am thus an ambivalent person — ambi-valent — two sided. I suspect I am not alone in this regard. Many of us aspire to be good persons. Yet we also feel and do things that we don't consider good. Maybe we all are ambivalent.

A classic statement of such ambivalence is found in the Christian New Testament, in Paul's Letter to the Galatians. Near the end of his letter he writes of an inner war between flesh and spirit. By flesh Paul does not mean the physical body and by spirit he does not mean a disembodied soul; he is referring to two sets of emotions and behaviors — two ways of being a person. The works of the flesh are "fornication, impurity, licentiousness, idolatry, sorcery, enmities, strife, jealously, anger, quarrels, dissensions, factions, envy, drunkenness, carousing, and things like these. . . . By contrast, the fruit of the Spirit is love, joy, peace, patience, kindness, generosity, faithfulness, gentleness, and self-control."[1]

I do not experience all the works of the flesh or the fruits of the Spirit in me, but I am aware of enough of them to think that Paul is describing the ambivalence I feel about myself. I am a two-sided creature, capable of good and bad feelings and of acting in helpful and harmful ways. Why am I capable of both? Why am I ambi-valent?

Part of the answer seems to lie in our evolved biological nature. Some of the emotions and behaviors described by Paul are portrayed by evolutionary psychologists as the result of evolution. In his book *The Moral Animal*, Robert Wright summarizes their findings and describes how humans might have evolved to be morally ambivalent.[2] Emotions such as anger, jealousy, and envy, along with behaviors such as promiscuity and quarreling have evolved because they offer some adaptive advantage, some increased chance for reproductive success. So too have evolved inclinations for love, patience, faithfulness, and peacemaking.

Such a view of moral ambivalence is supported by studies of our closest biological kin. Franz de Waal's *Good Natured* and Richard Wrangham and Dale Peterson's *Demonic Males*, when taken together, suggest that our ambivalence is rooted in a biological heritage that is also present to some extent in other primates. Wrangham and Peterson highlight chimpanzee lethal aggression and bonobo sexual liberality.[3] De Waal makes a case for the evolution of primate tendencies for sympathy, reciprocity, and peacemaking.[4] Depending on circumstances, all these morally ambivalent emotions and behaviors are biologically adaptive.

Victor Johnston expands this view by presenting evidence that our emotions are functions of different parts of our brains, especially that part called the limbic system or the old mammalian brain. According to Paul MacLean we have a triune brain. Evolutionarily, the oldest part is our brain stem, which we share with reptiles — our reptilian brain. Our newest part is the neocortex, which exists in varying degree in other animals but is most highly evolved in humans. In between but interconnected with the other parts is the limbic system. We share this part of our brain with other primates and mammals.[5]

Johnston, following MacLean, describes three functional subdivisions of the limbic system and their interconnections in humans with the motor areas of the brain stem on the one hand and the neocortex on the other.[6] One functional subdivision regulates emotional reactions concerned with self-preservation, such as fear and anger. Johnston suggests that these were probably naturally selected in animals "in response to other predators or other dangers that were consistently present in our evolutionary past."[7] This part of the limbic system is also the locus of behaviors and feelings associated with feeding. For example, the feeling of disgust may have evolved as a way of avoiding spoiled or rotten food, or other decaying substances that we now know indicate the presence of microorganisms and possible disease. Another part of the limbic system contributes to survival because it regulates sexual functions and feelings, such as feelings of sexual passion, that are conducive to mating. The third subdivision is concerned with feelings and behaviors that regulate maternal behavior and play, such as love for one's child and perhaps feelings of surprise at novel events.

As I read people like Wright, de Waal, Wrangham and Peterson, and Johnston, it all makes sense to me as I look at myself. It makes sense that I have evolved to be ambivalent with different parts of my brain functioning to enable a variety of emotions and behaviors in response to a variety of situations. For example, I love and trust my wife, but I also feel a tinge of jealousy that puts me on guard when she attends professional meetings with other men. I am sympathetic with most people regardless of who they are, but I sometimes envy those who are more accomplished than I am. I am usually friendly and peaceful, but when I feel threatened, I experience my aggressiveness rising. Biological evolution seems to have made me a mixed bag of emotions and behaviors, but all of them, expressed in the right places at the right times, help me survive and flourish as I encounter the promises and the threats of ever changing human and natural environments.

Another way to help understand our ambivalent nature is in terms of a model of human personality developed by family therapist Richard C. Schwartz. Drawing on twenty years of clinical experience, Schwartz suggests that as we grow up we develop an inner ecology.[8] We become a system of interacting parts. The parts represent constellations of beliefs, feelings, and behaviors as we respond to other people and to our wider environment. Schwartz calls these parts "exiles," "managers," and "firefighters." Usually, all these parts are good. They help a person respond effectively to a variety of life experiences. However, under traumatic or continual stress some parts can become extreme and polarized with one another. And some can take over our internal system in ways that are harmful to ourselves and to our relationships with others.

"Exiles" are the parts that carry feelings we don't want to feel. We become aware of our exiles when we feel sad, afraid, hurt, rejected, powerless, ashamed, hopeless, empty, and unlovable. Other parts function as our "managers." These try to keep order and control by being perfect, pleasing, or care taking in relation to others; by judging and criticizing other internal parts; and by intellectualizing, rationalizing, and denying. However, sometimes the exiled feelings can't be controlled by the managers, and they come pouring out. When this happens other parts spring into action. The "firefighters" try to extinguish the painful feelings or disconnect the person from them with such things as alcohol, drugs, food binges, sex binges, shopping binges, fantasy, too much sleeping, rage, violence, clinical depression, and suicidal thinking. But in trying to extinguish the painful feelings, the firefighters drive the person to act excessively, out of control. This happens until some kind of satisfaction is temporarily reached and a state of relative calm returns — until whatever is stressing the system again overruns the managers' control and the firefighters respond again.

Schwartz's internal family systems model resonates with my own experience. When I was a child my parents were wonderful in many ways. They especially encouraged me to grow and to think freely for myself. Yet, when they disciplined me, their mode of discipline was to separate me from them. If I acted up during our evening meal, they sent me to my room without the rest of supper. If I got too rambunctious in the back seat on a long car trip, and if their pleas for me to quiet down failed, they stopped the car and threatened to leave me beside the road. Perhaps as a result, in one of the earliest dreams I remember we were getting ready to go somewhere and I was dawdling. Suddenly my parents were not there. In my dream I rushed to the window, and they were driving away.

To this day I am aware of a part of myself — a little child part — that is afraid of being rejected and abandoned by those closest to me. I also am aware of other parts, my managing parts, urging me to keep busy, to get to work, or to make friends. I am aware that they are trying to keep my lonely part under control. But sometimes my managers aren't enough. Sometimes I feel overwhelmed, frustrated, discouraged, and lonely. This may happen after a class if the class did not go well. It may happen as I am having difficulty organizing my thoughts as I write a paper or a chapter of a book. When I become overwhelmed, I experience a firefighter coming to quench the flames of loneliness and worthlessness. I head to the refrigerator — for soothing food. A big dish of ice cream, and maybe a second dish. My anxious child part begins to feel better — at least for a little while.

So, as I try to be a good person, I find that I am ambivalent. I sometimes act in excessive ways that can be harmful to myself, and sometimes to others. I also see this happening in our society. I see people acting excessively — on binges of eating, drinking, and shopping. And I wonder whether this is one of the reasons why we are having so much trouble responding to our environmental crises.

I don't want to oversimplify. There are many reasons why we are having difficulty in responding to global environmental problems by living harmoniously with our natural world. I described some of these in chapter three, "Peril in the Global Village." Now I want to suggest one more. We are living in a stress-filled world. Every day we learn about new diseases, new outbreaks of political unrest, and other new threats to our lives and livelihood. Every day in our work and at home we are expected to live at a pace of life much faster than our early human ancestors. Our current social environment may be pushing us to live beyond what our evolved, early hominid brains are comfortable with. As we try to think fast and live fast-paced lives, there are times we become overwhelmed. Firefighters kick in. Some people react violently and destructively in anger. Others react acquisitively by consuming. Just as I head for the refrigerator, some head for the local bar or the shopping mall. We try to satisfy our fears of being inadequate and unworthy by consuming more and more material things. When we are environmentally aware, we know that this is problematic. We know we can't keep this up indefinitely. But our exiles are out of control, and we are trying to put out the inner flames of distress.

How then can we live more at peace with ourselves and more in tune with our social and natural worlds? How can we be more integrated, effective social-ecological selves? I think we have three resources that may help us. One is suggested by Richard Schwartz in his model of the person. A second is a capacity of our biologically evolved brains. A third is offered by a variety of religious traditions. These three resources all encourage us to seek our sacred center — a calm state of being fully awake in the present moment to all that is within and outside ourselves, a state of compassion for all within and outside, and a state of self-leadership that guides us to live more harmoniously with other people and the rest of the world.

In addition to exiles, managers, and firefighters, Schwartz's model of human persons holds that we have a core "self," which is not a substance but a felt experience.[9] It is a state in which we are calm and centered, peaceful yet energized, confident, curious, creative, and compassionate. It is a state of understanding without judging, connecting and not disengaging, healing and not hurting. It is being present and being in the present. When one is in this state of "being in self," according to Schwartz, one exercises compassionate leadership with all of one's parts. One engages in an internal, sympathetic conversation with them to uncover what they need and what they are trying to accomplish. One guides the parts toward supportive interactions with one another, so that they all contribute to the good of the whole person in healthy relationships with others.

The psychological state of being in self, of being present and in the present, is supported by our biologically evolved brains, by what Antonio Damasio calls our "core self." In his book *The Feel-*

ing of What Happens: Body and Mind in the Making of Consciousness, Damasio suggests that we have three selves, each made possible because of the activity of different regions of our brains.[10] The first is the "proto-self," which is an interconnected, moment by moment coherent collection of neural patterns that represent and regulate the internal state of the organism. It is unconscious; we are not aware of our proto-selves. The second is the "core self," which is generated when a human being interacts with an object, which can be either outside or inside the person. This object-organism interaction generates a nonverbal account of the object and its relation to the individual. This account includes the person's feeling of him or herself knowing the object. It is a present-moment experience of awareness of self and other — a feeling of oneself in the process of feeling what happens. Damasio's third self is what he calls the "autobiographical self," which is based on memories of multiple past experiences in images that are recalled or reconstructed. As we remember narratives of ourselves from the past, we gain a sense of our identity over time.

Schwartz and Damasio describe the human person from two different frameworks, one based on psychological clinical experience and the other based on laboratory and clinical brain research. Therefore, one cannot find exact correlations between their ideas. Yet, it does seem to me that Damasio's autobiographical self is where one finds the exiles, managers, and firefighters in Schwartz's internal system. Although some of features of these parts are grounded in our evolved brains, how they come to work in our lives is the result of life experiences and ways of coping we have developed in response to our experiences. It also seems to me that Damasio's core self exhibits features of Schwartz's "being in self." In both, one is focused on the present moment, on what is going on inside and outside of one's person in a state of interconnection between self and other. Schwartz adds to Damasio's conception the idea of compassionate self-leadership, which gives a sense of the core self as not only responding to objects but as guiding one's internal states that come forward into the present from the autobiographical self.

What is the point of all this for our living? I think it is that both Schwartz and Damasio suggest that when we are in our core selves, we are mindful of all that is going on and also of ourselves as present in the midst of all that is going on. Each seems to suggest what I am calling our sacred center — a center from which the various parts of ourselves can be harmonized, in which the ambivalences in our nature can be constructively interrelated.

Religions have different names for what I am calling our sacred center. It is referred to as Soul, Spirit, Image of God, Christ Nature, Mind of Christ, Buddha Nature, Atman in Hinduism, Jiva in Jainism, and God Consciousness. These names point to a state of mind that is centered, calm, creative, and compassionate — present fully in the moment for oneself and for others. Out of such a state can come healing within oneself and in one's relationships with others.

One of my favorite analogies of this state is expressed in the *Katha Upanishad*, one of the philosophical writings that are the concluding section of the sacred Hindu texts called the *Vedas*. "Know that the Self is the rider, the body the chariot; that the intellect is the charioteer, and the mind the reins. The senses, say the wise, are the horses; the roads they travel are the mazes of desire. The wise call the Self the enjoyer when he is united with the body, the senses, and the mind."[11] What strikes me about this passage is that the self is not the intellect, the active, rational part of a human being, as is often thought in Western philosophy. The self is a state of being along for the ride, so to speak, as other parts of the person perform their tasks. The self is thus the mindful observer of all that is happening.

I find it relatively easy to put myself into this state. For example, I can feel myself "stepping back" inside my head somewhere behind my eyes as I am typing this paragraph. I then become more clearly aware of the process of typing — thoughts forming, hands moving, keys clicking, and words appearing on the screen. I can do the same when I'm walking, talking, reading, cooking, cleaning, washing dishes, lying down, and visiting with others. From inside my head (in my chariot) I calmly view all that is happening to me and all that I'm doing. In this state, I become relaxed, peaceful, and content — fully in the present moment, awake to everything. I am the "rider in the chariot" of my mind-body as it interacts with the world.

Religions have developed a variety of practices to help bring us into such a state. Many involve meditation. A simple exercise is suggested by the contemporary Buddhist monk Thich Nhat Hanh. He says that "conscious breathing is the most basic Buddhist practice for touching peace," and he offers the following short exercise:

> Breathing in, I calm my body.
> Breathing out, I smile.
> Dwelling in the present moment,
> I know this is a wonderful moment.

He then shortens this to: "As we breath in, we say to ourselves 'Calming,' and as we breath out, we say 'Smiling.' As we breath in again, we say 'Present moment,' and as we breath out, 'Wonderful moment.'"[12]

What do such exercises in mindfulness do for us? Thich Nhat Hanh writes: "When we are mindful, touching deeply the present moment, we can see and listen deeply, and the fruits are always understanding, acceptance, love, and the desire to relieve suffering and bring joy. When our beautiful child comes up to us and smiles, we are completely there for her."[13] He also writes: "The most precious gift we can offer others is our presence. When our mindfulness embraces those we love, they will bloom like flowers. If you love someone but rarely make yourself available to him or her, that is not true love.... When you are really there, showing your loving-kindness and understanding, the energy of the Holy Spirit is in you."[14] Or we might say the Buddha nature is in us. Or, with Schwartz, we are in self-leadership. We are in our sacred center.

How then can I be a good person? How can I live as one who is friendly, loving, caring, compassionate, curious, open to new possibilities, intelligent, and wise? How can I live this way in light of my ambivalent nature, attested to by evolutionary theory and by therapists like Richard Schwartz? The answer is simple to state but more difficult to live: it is to be fully in the present moment as I encounter others, as I encounter all my parts in my autobiographical self, as I encounter all forms of life, streams, rocks, and stars. In this state of consciousness called my sacred center, I have little need to acquire material things — only what I need for nourishment and life support. Being mindful of the ever changing succession of present moments, I can enjoy the richness of nature, human relationships, and my inner self. In a state of constant mindfulness I can live in peace and love in our wonderful evolving world — in the dance of the sacred.

✍ Chapter 14 ✍

In Harmony with Cruciform Nature

Growing up in mid-twentieth-century America, I learned to think of the natural world as something to be enjoyed, used, and even conquered. As a child I enjoyed winter sledding and skating. I saw cows being milked to provide me with food. I learned how to control nature by mowing lawns and tending gardens. What I did not learn until much later, actually not much before I turned fifty, was to value nature for its own sake.

In my studies of philosophy, religion, and science, I have come to understand some of the roots of my attitudes toward the natural world. The root that goes deepest into the past is dualism, a dualism that separates good from evil, identifies the natural world with evil, and says we must escape from or conquer the material world. This set of attitudes probably originated with the ancient Iranian prophet Zoroaster. Zoroaster reformed the older polytheistic traditions of his society into a monotheism that worshiped Ahura Mazda, the "Wise Lord." Although Ahura Mazda expressed his will though his Holy Spirit, he was opposed by the lying "Evil Spirit," Angra Mainyu. The universe thus became the scene of eternal combat between two principles, one good, one evil. Ultimately Ahura Mazda would be victorious. Meanwhile, humans needed to understand that the conflict between good and evil in their own lives reflected the warfare between these two primary cosmic realities.[1] Such thinking came through Judaism into early Christianity as the warfare between God and Satan. Ultimately God would triumph, and human beings were called to be on the right side at God's final victory and judgment of good and evil.

When Christianity incorporated Greek philosophy into its thinking, another dualistic element was added — that between spirit and matter. Spirit, mind, and reason (often seen as male) were eternally good while matter, emotions, and instincts (often seen as female) were understood as opposed to and threatening to spiritual well-being. Hence they were evil, a part of the world that Thomas à Kempis described as a place where one could get lost on the way to one's eternal, heavenly destination.[2] In the battle between good and evil, one way to attain victory was to escape Earth to a heavenly realm. In the context of moral and metaphysical dualism, the idea that one could at death escape life's limits gave people hope and guidance, especially at a time when humans were relatively powerless to change their earthly lives for the better.

With the beginnings of European colonialism and the rise of modern science and technology, there was added to this otherworldly kind of Christianity an emphasis on conquering and taming this world. The Puritan colonists in New England, who were educated and civilized Europeans, saw as a part of their mission the taming of the American wilderness. Religious historian Catherine Albanese writes that the Puritans "often understood nature in negative terms. It was mostly wilderness, and only occasionally with a great deal of human cultivation it became a garden.... The wilderness was a place inhabited by wild beasts and nameless terrors. It was a place to which civilization has not penetrated, out of control, like teeming forests and the dense vegetation."[3] Two centuries after the Puritans, Lyman Beecher was raising money to support the funding of education on the frontier, west of the Appalachian Mountains. He called people to participate in the great work of conquering the wilderness:

> No people in the same time ever performed so great a work as has already been performed in the West. Such an extent of forest never fell before the arm of man in forty years, and gave place, as by enchantment to such an empire of cities, towns, and villages, and agriculture, and merchandise, and manufactures, and roads, and rapid navigation, and schools, and colleges, and libraries, and literary enterprise, with such a relative amount of religious influence, as has been produced

by the spontaneous effort of the religious denominations of the West....[4]

Such a view of conquering wild nature was supported by the mechanistic world view of modern science. Drawing on Newtonian physics and conceiving God as the designer and maker of a natural, machinelike world, much Enlightenment scientific philosophy came to view nature as something to be manipulated, controlled, and used as a tool for human welfare.

This religious, scientific, philosophical view was the one I absorbed from my culture. It shaped my own thinking — my cultural self. I did not question it until I began to read about how other cultures thought of the relation between humanity and nature. One anecdote I read typifies a way of thinking that is an alternative to dualism. A Taoist philosopher, commenting on the climbing of Mount Everest said: "When you Westerners climb Mount Everest, you say, 'We have conquered Mount Everest.' However, we Taoists would say, 'We have befriended Mount Everest.' "[5] A Taoist conceives of humans and nature as united, in harmony with one another, a view that stands in sharp contrast to what has been the prevalent thinking in the West — a dualist, conquest mentality.

When I presented a paper at the 1988 World Academic Conference of the Seoul Olympiad on science, religion, and the environment, one of my fellow presenters was the Buddhist monk Bup Jung. Like the Taoist quoted above, Bup Jung developed a "harmony view" of our relationship with nature. His paper began:

> I often recall the words of a youngster from a few summers ago, who had come with his father from Seoul to visit the mountains where I dwell. "Papa, the breeze is sweet!" Then, drinking gulps of water drawn from the well in his hand, he exclaimed, "Ah, it's delicious, truly delicious." Recollections of this five-year-old's precocious comments echo in my ears to this day.
>
> Sweet breeze! How direct and poetic an expression, compared to the cliched descriptions of fresh and clear. Years of drinking water distilled by the fumes of chemicals must have enhanced the flavor of the mineral water springing from

the mountains. This is why children, pure, transparent and innocent, are "the father of man."

Who has stolen the "sweet breeze" from our youngsters? Who has adulterated our delicious water? Nature only preserves itself, never destroying. Man, civilized humans have harmed and defiled nature. The processes of disorderly industrialization and urbanization have polluted the fresh water and clean air. Seduced by excessive materialism, man has forgotten the natural privileges bestowed on him by nature and the environment, and is destroying his benefactor.

Bup Jung's paper continued:

Nature provides man with those elements essential to the physical and spiritual sustenance without any demand whatsoever in return. The relationship closely resembles a merciful mother who grants her child all that she can without a second thought.

Nature to us humans is not only an eternal mother but a great teacher as well. There is an inherent order within itself, which is manifested in many forms. With spring, summer, fall and winter we witness the order of seasons, as there is order in harvesting when the farmer reaps what he sows. Rain quenches the thirst of droughts, and even endless floods are put to an end. Winds set free restrained elements, and continuous flux prevents spoil. Darkness descends on the bright day to relieve the fatigue accumulated from industry. Man must learn to obey the rules and order of nature. Simultaneously, we must learn from nature how to live a natural life. This is because that which is natural is concurrently healthy.

Bup Jung's paper concluded:

There is need for a new relationship between man and nature to be established, not one of conquest and exploitation but one of cooperation and companionship.[6]

At the Seoul conference I and everyone else agreed that humans should learn to live in harmony with nature. Yet, in some ways

I found the views of Bup Jung and others problematic. I tried to express my problem with this view by asking: "What is the nature with which we should be in harmony?" I pointed out that Bup Jung's way is not the only way to describe nature. Nature can be brutal as well as beautiful. Evolutionary biologist George Williams, following in the tradition of Thomas Henry Huxley, states that, when viewed from the perspective of what humans intuitively regard as moral, nature is immoral.[7] There is evidence in the animal kingdom of selfishness, rape, murder, deception, cuckoldry, infanticide, cannibalism, and so on. Further, when we look at our own human, biologically evolved predispositions, we have the capacity to be jealous, deceitful, and spiteful as well as friendly, helpful, loving, and peaceful.

Underlying the outward harmony, one can find a picture of nature that is closer to the dualistic, conquest view. Among various species predators eat prey, parasites feed on hosts, and males and females try to outsmart one another in the reproductive game. One can also find examples of cooperation, of symbiotic relationships between species. If nature is our teacher, which aspects of nature should we try to imitate — the sweetness of the air and the harmony of the ebb and flow of natural cycles, or the struggle for survival, using whatever means we can to reproduce and further our kind? Being in harmony with nature can mean either cooperation or competition, either befriending or conquering.

I think that each view of nature I have outlined, the dualistic, conquest view and the harmony view, has some truth — but not the whole truth. These views need to be reconciled as part of a single understanding. Competition and cooperation, conquest and harmony are the yang and yin of a larger picture, a more complete understanding of nature and its value.

In constructing this larger picture I follow the thinking of Holmes Rolston III.[8] Like many moral philosophers, Rolston writes about intrinsic and instrumental value. In addition, he also develops the idea of systemic value, the value of an entire system as a productive process. He further suggests that all three kinds of value are not just the ways in which human engage in valuing. They are ways of valuing found in the natural world apart from humans. The notion of systemic value, the value of productive processes, I suggest is the value of the creative process. This value links us to the divine. We explored its significance in chapter nine, "Our Natural Family."

Intrinsic, instrumental, and creative value apply to both humans and the rest of the natural world. Recognizing this fact helps establish harmony between humans and the rest of nature — a harmony that is a solidarity in suffering and death as well as joy and life. Intrinsic value means that something is valuable for its own sake, in and of itself. All organisms — humans, animals, plants, and microorganisms — affirm the value of their own lives. Although humans can think about their own value and along with other animals feel their own value, the primary way all organisms affirm their own worth is biologically. We all simply live and, when threatened, struggle to continue to live. Whether conscious or not, whether felt or not, the struggle for life is a sign that an organism is affirming is own worth.

It is ironic that some say that affirming oneself is selfish and is therefore immoral. How can it be immoral to value one's own being, to struggle to do all one can to live? Unless one continues to affirm oneself, one will not live. From the perspective of Rolston's environmental ethics, valuing one's own being is not wrong, either for humans or for other species of plants and animals.

As each individual organism does what it needs to do in order to live, it uses other elements of the natural world to sustain itself. It thereby treats others as having instrumental value, as being useful to its own continuation and fulfillment. Plants use sunlight, oxygen, water, and minerals from the soil to produce sugars for their nourishment and growth. Many animals eat plants for food. In doing so, they are in Rolston's terms "capturing value," acquiring what is of value in the plants for their own life support. Some animals capture life support value by preying on other animals. Various kinds of microorganisms do the same, preying on plants and animals, including humans. Bacteria that infect us and make us miserable, and even sometimes threaten our lives, are simply trying to capture the instrumental value we have for them, so that they can live and reproduce. We humans do the same. We feed on plants and animals, killing them, destroying the value they have for themselves and thereby gaining their instrumental value for our own life support.

We don't think there is anything wrong with plants capturing the value of sunlight and carbon dioxide. Neither do we worry about animals and humans eating plants, destroying the lives of some individual specimens. However, many of us become troubled when animals feed on animals. We also become troubled when microorganisms feed on other things — calling it disease. One reason why we are so troubled is that animals and humans can experience pain and suffering when they are captured or invaded by others seeking a source of food. However, the pain is not produced just by the predator capturing its prey. What is primarily responsible for the pain and suffering are developments in the nervous systems of the animals and humans being consumed. Pain and suffering are actually part of the defense system sentient creatures have, so that they will try to defend themselves, continuing to affirm the value of their own being. Pain and suffering are the price paid for the evolution of feeling and sense experiencing in animals, and of abstract thinking in humans. We wouldn't want to do away with these. We value feelings, sense experiences, and thought — even though they give rise to pain and suffering when other creatures use us instrumentally as they too try to live.

Is all this cooperation or competition, harmony or conquest? To say it is one or the other is too simple. What we are looking for is a kind of dynamic harmony, at times a paradoxical harmony. This view of harmony affirms the intrinsic value of all living things and it also recognizes that, in order to have intrinsic value, each organism must "feed" off of other forms of existence, sometimes destroying them. However, as something is destroyed — whether a quantum of sunlight, an atom of oxygen, a molecule of water, a plant, an animal, a human being — it becomes transformed as part of another. It furthers the life of another. This is a more comprehensive kind of harmony, not the peaceful harmony of sweet breezes — the gas molecules of which also become transformed as we inhale them. It is not just the harmony of sunsets and sunrises, of shorter and longer days, of seasons of the years. It is the harmony of a dance of life and death, of growth and decay, of pleasure and pain, of tranquility and suffering. It is the harmony of the dancing Hindu deity Shiva, who continually creates, destroys, and recreates all aspects of the universe. This dynamic, dialectical harmony is the core of the third kind of value — the productive or creative value inherent in the interactions of all things.

All individual things are a part of larger, dynamic systems. When Rolston develops the idea of productive or creative value, he does so by discussing ecosystems. Ecosystems are the creative matrices that produce intrinsic value as they create new species. Calling ecosystems creative matrices indicates the significance of the interactions among organisms and between organisms and the nonliving environment. It is these interactions that create new forms of life as existing life forms reproduce, genetically vary, and contribute to the selection pressure on one another. To recognize that an ecosystem is a creative matrix is to focus on the processes of evolution as the source of much ongoing life and of new life.

However, new species are often created at the expense of the old. As organisms mutate and as some mutations are more successfully reproduced, the modified or new organisms often "win" over the old in the game of reproductive success. According to Rolston, new creation at the expense of older created things occurs most dramatically in wilderness areas where there is a great diversity of species.

> The wilderness can seem a great scene of disorder, but it is also a scene of the pumping out of disorder. . . . The marvel is how dirt spontaneously assembled into Cambrian worms, later into Cretaceous opossums, and still later into . . . persons. The degradation of things in the wild is followed by nature's orderly self-assembling of new creatures amidst this perpetual perishing. Earth slays her children, a seeming great disvalue, but bears an annual crop in their stead. This prolife generative impulse is the most startling and valuable miracle of all.[9]

Rolston's productive value is nothing less than what I have earlier portrayed as the creative process, the divine that is ever present in the world. As a result of this most fundamental kind of value, the earth exhibits a tendency toward ever increasing diversity of life forms. These forms of life or species become a part of the creative process itself, even as they are valuable in their own right and even as they become instrumentally valuable in supporting the lives of others. However, as valuable as they are, species do not last forever. Biologists estimate that 99 percent of the species of our planet are now extinct. Nonetheless, in the midst of massive death the long-term result is a proliferation of life. "Over evolutionary time nature has rendered most of her kinds extinct, only to generate others in their places, gradually increasing from zero to five or ten million species. This constructive tendency, little understood and mysterious, must in some sense be a good thing. Humans are an end result of it, as is the wonderland Earth."[10]

Extinction and creation. Death and new birth. There is harmony in nature, and humans are a part of that harmony. However, this harmony is achieved only in a process of creating and sustaining life in which death leads to new birth, in which life becomes food, at times painfully, for other life. What we humans must "value in nature is an ecology, a pregnant Earth, a projective and prolife system in which . . . individuals can prosper but are also sacrificed indifferently to their pains and pleasures, individual well-being a lofty but passing role in a storied natural history. From the perspective of individuals there is violence, struggle, death; but from a systems perspective, there is also harmony, interdependence, and ever-continuing life."[11]

How can we represent to ourselves this interweaving of suffering and death with creativity and life? One way is to look for concrete symbols that interpret a broad range of our experience. When I look at the ambivalence of the creative, evolutionary process that I have suggested is the dance of the sacred, I consider the Christian symbol of the cross and Holmes Rolston's suggestion that evolving nature may be regarded as if it were cruciform.[12]

Each religion has central symbols that help us see more clearly and completely the fundamental nature of things. The family is such a symbol in both Native American and Confucian thought. The human family symbolizes the kinship of all creation. The symbol of the Tao as yang and yin is another such symbol, showing the dynamic interplay between opposites in tension in the natural world and human life. The cross of Christianity is still another. It represents the suffering of the Holy in the midst of humanity, a suffering that is redemptive, bringing about new good for others. The cross symbolizes that the fundamental ground of all being has as one of its features, suffering. It opens up a window to the way things are — a window through which we see redemptive suffering as part and parcel of the nature of the world in which we live.[13]

In a 1994 essay in *Zygon: Journal of Religion and Science*, Rolston asks, "Does nature need to be redeemed?"

> If redemption means being saved from the guilt of sin, then fauna, flora, rocks, and rivers have no guilt and cannot be redeemed. If redemption means being saved from the consequences of sin, then nature can be redeemed only so far as it has been ruined by human sin that infects the natural course.... If redemption can mean that there is a transformation by which the destruction of the old, lower life is not really destruction but renovation, the creation of newer, higher levels of life, then our inquiry is promising indeed.[14]

Later he points out that "the question is not whether the world is, or ever was, a happy place. Rather, the question is whether it is a place of significant suffering through to something higher."[15] Then he suggests that, among other things, nature is cruciform.

I do not agree with Rolston that suffering needs to lead to something higher in order to be redemptive. I think it too difficult to determine whether some new species, some new aspect of culture, some new pattern of living realized through suffering is higher than what went before. However, I think we can say that when some new good emerges through a process that involves suffering then the loss of the old and its accompanying pain and sorrow are redeemed in the new.

How then can we live in harmony with nature? It is not simply living peacefully with sweet breezes and fresh water, although keeping air pure and water clean is certainly worthwhile. It does not mean promoting death, destruction, pain, and suffering. These are part of evolving nature, but we do not need to add more unnecessarily. However, when death, pain, and suffering do occur, living in harmony with nature means being open to new possibilities for good to which they might lead. A fundamental aspect of nature is that it is cruciform. Living in harmony with cruciform nature means being open to the possibilities of new life, new truth, new beauty, and new love that emerge in the midst of suffering.

Chapter 15

From Life to Love

For much of my professional life I have lived in my mind, exploring new possibilities for thinking about God, myself, immortality, and how I could live morally and meaningfully in a scientific, pluralistic age. A few years ago, I was faced with a personal crisis that has transformed me. During the crisis, I discovered that the naturalistic, evolutionary theology I have been describing helped me interpret what was happening and gave me direction regarding what to do. That theology also underwent a transformation. What had been an intellectual activity became integrated with my feelings and actions.

In this and the next chapter I will share details of some personal experiences and feelings. I hope that doing this will help you see how my theological theorizing became concrete living. I also hope that my experiences will enable you to use your own similar, yet different, experiences to see if the ideas we have been exploring might be helpful to you.

One of my favorite religious songs, sung often in my church, is "Spirit of Life" by Carolyn McDade.

> Spirit of Life, come unto me.
> Sing in my heart all the stirrings of compassion.
> Blow in the wind, rise in the sea;
> Move in the hand, giving life the shape of justice.
> Roots hold me close; wings set me free;
> Spirit of Life, come to me, come to me.[1]

On December 23, 1993, I was visited not by the spirit of life, but by the spirit of death. Carol and I had been married thirty-three years. Now her life and our life together were predicted to end.

We sat in the oncologist's office. He spent an hour and a half with us, gently describing Carol's rare form of stomach cancer, which had already metastasized to her lymph system. He said that only 1 percent of the people with this kind of cancer lived longer than a year. The usual prognosis was six months.

Was there anything that could be done? Even the most aggressive form of chemotherapy might prolong her life another six months. But she would have to deal with the affects of treatment. The choice was between almost sure death with no attempt to curb the multiplying cells, or almost sure death with a little more time together.

The doctor went to get his nurse, who would explain to us the variety of medical, social, and personal resources available at the Orlando Cancer Center. When left alone, Carol and I broke down and cried. As we held each other tightly, I said, "You're leaving me, Honey!" Even as I put these words on paper several years later, they bring tears to my eyes. They are an expression of one of my worst fears, of being left alone, cut off from those I love. Little did I realize then how our love would grow even as her life ebbed away. We were just beginning a journey — from life to love.

During the coming months I learned much about cancer. One of the things I came to realize was that cancer cells are an example of Darwinian evolution. The cells of our bodies mutate all the time. At any one time, we have about two thousand cancer cells in our bodies, but our immune system detects and eliminates them. Random variations and natural selection occur not just in the transmission of genes from one generation to the next. They occur within the confines of our own bodies.

Theologically, this means for me that I cannot regard cancer as evil, even though it caused suffering and death for me and someone I love. Cancer is simply a manifestation of the very same processes involved in evolution. Some genetic changes lead to new forms of life. However, the vast majority of biological mutations lead to malfunctioning organisms, sterility, and death. The results of the cell changes in our bodies that cause runaway cell growth can create suffering and death. But the system of evolution that embodies constant change also has created our living planet, our species, ourselves. The dance of life is also the dance of death. The spirit of life is also the spirit of death.

Try as we might to treat and cure disease, to preserve the intrinsic value of a life, sometimes we cannot ward off death. Death is just as natural as life. Sickness is just as natural as health. However, we can make a difference in how we respond to events that bring about disease and death. They ravish and destroy our bodies. We can't do much about that. What we can do something about is whether they also ravish and destroy our spirit. Here we have a choice. It depends on how well we are able to discern new opportunities for living, even in the midst of dying.

Death is tragic, and it often occurs with much suffering and loss. However, death also opens up new opportunities for living. I first became aware of this when Jack died of cancer. Jack was a close friend, a father figure to me. He was a scientist, a physician. In fact, he had three medical careers, as a surgeon, a psychiatrist, and a dermatologist. As a scientifically minded person Jack studied the causes of his cancer, and he gave a lecture on it to our church. He wanted to learn how it had come about. He said, "I want to get to know my murderer."

After his death, my fatherly friend continued to live in my mind. I remembered his lecture on how his cancer was killing him. And I wasn't satisfied. I was left with a medical understanding of how his condition and his death had come about. However, that was not what I was seeking. I was asking not only "How?" but "Why?" Not "why" in a causative sense but why in the sense, "What is the significance of this?" and "Where do I go from here?" I was looking for meaning and moral guidance out of this experience.

Two ideas came to mind. One was from astrophysics. In *Cosmic Dawn*, Eric Chaisson illustrates that things have to die so that new things can be born. For example, stars die. They go through their main sequence, burning hydrogen and fusing it into helium, until they use up all their fuel. They then go through a series of expansions and contractions until the giant stars explode in supernovae, and out of the death of these stars heavier elements are created. These become the star dust out of which new stars and planets, such as our own are born. Death leads to birth. Then I thought of the Christian story of crucifixion and resurrection. For me it is a symbol that in dying new possibilities for living arise. I also thought of the fact that founders of religions, or social movements, some-times contribute as much by their dying as by their living. Death opens up new possibilities for life. Death contributes to making all things new.

Such was the case with Jack's death. Now that he was gone, his wife, his family, and his friends had to be open to new possibilities for living. That was our challenge, because dying and death also opened up possibilities for further diminishment of our personalities, of our relationships with each other — a loss of the spiritual as well as the physical — a second kind of death. Still, to me the message is clear. Even in the midst of grief and loss, possibilities for new truth, new love, new life are present. It is up to us to discern and follow them.

While my friend's death helped me to see the importance of dis-cerning new opportunities for something good after death, Carol's dying tutored me in finding possibilities for good in the midst of dying. This was possible because of her realistic, yet positive, re-sponse to the news of her terminal illness. Her initial reaction to our oncologist's report was, "I'm not afraid to die. In the time I have left I want to do as much as I can, and someone has to be in that 1 percent. Why not me?" So our medical, spiritual adventure began.

At the beginning I said to myself — only to myself, "How am I going to get through this?" As people told us, the answer was to "take one day at a time." So I took off from work and spent all my time with Carol. We revisited all the tourist sites in central Florida. We spent a lot of time with friends. We continued to be active in the new congregation we had helped found only a year earlier. We explored some alternative medical treatments and mind-body medicine. After five months Carol's stomach ceased to function and she could no longer eat. She elected to follow her oncologist's suggestion and have a feeding tube installed into her upper intestine. It was one of the few things our doctors could do. They had given us almost no hope of surviving, but they continued to offer us any treatment we needed to maintain the quality of life. With the tube she lived until March 20, 1995 — fifteen months after her cancer was discovered.

Because we had no hope of life, we experienced a strange kind of freedom. It was the freedom of knowing that the worst was going to happen, so we could do whatever we wanted. We did all the things mentioned above and more. Most important, we talked. We reviewed our life together. We enjoyed remembering the good times and we came to terms with all the trouble we had caused one another. We talked, we listened, we forgave. As life was ebbing away, love was growing.

In what we shared together we both became transformed. Carol, who was an extrovert, a person on the go, always doing, learned just to be. She learned to sit in her lazy-boy on the porch, being nourished by me through her feeding tube, and looking out at our yard and lake. One day she was rewarded. She saw an eagle drop out of the sky into the lake, catch a fish, and fly with it right over our house.

And I learned to love and be loved — in ways I never thought possible. Because I knew it could not last forever, I gave myself totally to caring for her. In the end she aged twenty years in fifteen months and my love became like that of an adult child for an aged parent. In the end she became dependent, even for walking, and my love was like a parent for a toddling child. And even as she became more dependent physically, she remained emotionally mature — expressing love to all whom she met, and especially to me. Every night, before she went to sleep, she looked into my eyes and said, "Thank you for everything!" Her deep gratitude lovingly consoled me in the midst of our loss.

I do not wish these experiences on anyone. But I know that when life goes, love can flourish. I know that love is more important than life.

Two years after Carol died, I was teaching New Testament at Rollins College. My students and I were discussing the ending of the Gospel of Mark. Most scholars think that Mark's Gospel ends not in triumph — not with clear, new good coming out of great evil. Instead it ends with death, an empty tomb, a muted promise for an unknown future, and confusion. When Mary Magdalene, Mary the mother of James, and Salome were told that Jesus had risen and gone to Galilee, instead of going to tell the disciples, "they went out and fled from the tomb, for terror and amazement had seized them; and they said nothing to anyone, for they were afraid."[2] What a way for the earliest written gospel to end. After the great detail in describing the trial, suffering, and death of Jesus, so little is offered as a promise for the future.

When I discussed this with my students, I suggested that maybe the point was not to look to the future for redemption from suffering. Certainly the readers of Mark, most likely facing suffering and death from Roman persecution, could not yet see that far. Maybe the point was that one could find saving good even in the midst of suffering, even in the face of death. That is indeed what I had discovered during the dying of my wife.

I would not wish suffering and death on anyone. But the universe seems to be so constituted that one cannot separate creation from destruction, pleasure from pain, joy from sorrow. In the midst of destruction new seeds of existence are being sown. In the midst of pain pleasure can be found. In the center of sorrow there can be profound joy. Even during the dying of a loved one, new love can be born.

My experience of being visited with the spirit of death leads me to want to rephrase Carolyn McDade's lovely and moving poetic song. Now, even after the spirit of a life has gone, I still can sing: "Spirit of Love, come unto me. Sing in my heart.... Blow in the wind.... Move in the hand.... Roots hold me close; wings set me free; Spirit of *Love*, come to me, come to me." The spirit of life may give way to the spirit of death — but love can still grow and flourish in remarkable ways.

✐ Chapter 16 ✑

Forsaken by God

One way that traditional religions have characterized the sacred center of our existence is with the word "love." "God is love." Often this means that there is a personal being who loves us. However, this idea is challenged by the experience of suffering in the world and in our own lives. The challenge also is for those who think, as I do, that the sacred is a process of creation. As we have seen, this process involves suffering and death in nature and in human life. If the process of creation is sacred, and also involves suffering and death, what does it mean to affirm that the sacred is love?

In my own life I have discovered that in the midst of dying and death, depending on how we choose to respond, love can grow. From the perspective of a naturalistic, evolutionary theology, one can say that at the heart of human life and in the midst of death the power of love can become manifest. Yet there is more. It also seems that love can die, only to be born again, transformed into new, expanding love. This for me is the meaning of that awful cry, uttered two thousand years ago from a cross outside Jerusalem: "My God, my God, why have you forsaken me?"[1]

Jesus of Nazareth is one of a small number of people who have catalyzed a major transformation in human history. Yet we don't know very much about him. We don't even know what he looked like, so that artists have been able to portray him in the likeness of their own people. We don't know much about his life. He had a public career of one to three years, but the record of this is sketchy. A contemporary historian cannot write much of a biography. Yet, this person was the fountainhead of a movement that has become one of the great religions of the world. Who was he?

Huston Smith suggests that we have to look at the meager record of Jesus' life in such a way that we can discern his character. What *kind* of person was he? One capsule summary is given by Peter. When asked to describe Jesus, Peter put it in one sentence: "He went about doing good."[2] He went about teaching, healing, caring for and being with those who were outcasts from society, who lived in despair. He did this with such single-mindedness that those who followed him began to think that if the God who created the world and who led the people of Israel out of bondage in Egypt took human form, perhaps this is what God would be like.

In the character of Jesus one finds an expression of the divine that people understood as undiscriminating love — love that knew no bounds, love for everyone, in every condition. Smith writes:

> Through the pages of the Gospels Jesus emerges as a man of strength and integrity who bore, as someone has said, no strangeness at all save the strangeness of perfection. He liked people and they liked him in turn. They loved him; they loved him intensely and they loved him in numbers. Drawn to him not only for his charismatic powers but for the compassion they sensed in him as well, they surrounded him, flocked about him, followed him. . . . People responded to Jesus, but equally he responded to them. He felt their appeal, whether they were rich or poor, young or old, saints or sinners. We have seen that he ignored the barriers that mores erected between people. He loved children. He hated injustice because of what it did to those he called, tenderly, "the least of these" (Matthew 25:40). Above all he hated hypocrisy, because it hid people from themselves and precluded the authenticity he sought to build into relationships. In the end it seemed to those who knew him best that here was a man in whom the human ego had disappeared, leaving his life so completely under the will of God that it was transparent to that will. It came to the point where they felt that as they looked at Jesus they were looking at something resembling God in human form.[3]

How can we understand such a person in a scientific age? Using evolutionary theory we can develop an analogy between biological and cultural evolution. In biology there are random variations in the

genetic codes of organisms. These give rise in particular environments to organisms that are more or less successful in reproducing
themselves. Those that are successful survive — natural selection.
Something similar holds for cultures. Although the mechanisms are
different, in cultures one finds that the patterns of tradition are
always varying. As they are transmitted from generation to generation, individual and small groups accidentally or intentionally
modify what has been handed down. Sometimes these variations
occur predominately in the lives of individuals — Confucius, Sid-
dhartha Gautama (the Buddha), Moses, Muhammad, and Jesus.
These are only a few examples of new changes in culture that have
survived. No doubt countless others did not survive. Even at the
time of Jesus, in the turmoil during the Roman empire, there were
other cultural mutations in the form of powerful healers, miracle
workers, and charismatic teachers. We have evidence of a few of
these, such as the Jewish holy men Hanina ben Dosa and Honi the
"circle drawer," and the pagan holy man and Pythagorean teacher
Apollonius of Tyana.[4]

Jesus' undiscriminating love was a cultural mutation. It was a love
so pervasive and powerful that it transformed the lives of many he
touched. Some came to believe that he was the Messiah, the one
sent by God to save his people from oppression — political, economic, and social oppression and well as the oppression of disease
and death. However, others regarded him as a threat to their beliefs and practices. He spoke with his own authority and challenged
the interpretation of the religious law of his day. He claimed to be
intimate with God, saying *Abba* — "Daddy." And some thought he
was fomenting revolution against the Romans. After a few years of
teaching, healing, and gathering a crowd of followers, this charismatic leader was brought to trial, condemned to death, and crucified
(the Roman capital punishment of the day). In evolutionary terms
he was a rejected, cultural mutation — selected against.

We all know that this was not the end. If it had been, Christianity
would not have become a major world religion. However, Christians
today sometimes move too quickly to the Resurrection, the rebirth
of Jesus in the minds and hearts of his followers, the power of his
spirit in their communal lives. It is all too easy to overlook that awful

cry from the cross: "My God, my God, why hast Thou forsaken me?" How could the Word become flesh have ever spoken that? What was the agony that was being expressed? Certainly the physical agony was great. But can that explain such a cry? I think that woven into the physical agony was a spiritual agony. It is the agony experienced when love dies, when a person whose character consists of love can no longer love. For when death comes to someone whose whole life is characterized by loving, when that person is mocked, scorned, and rejected — even left by his closest followers — that person must experience not just physical agony but an agony of the spirit. Love can no longer love. Love has been forsaken. God has been forsaken by God in a divine self-contradiction.

It has been a number of years since my wife Carol died, since our remarkable medical and spiritual journey, since the time when I came to share with her the depths of love. I still feel the beauty and the agony of that sacred time. From time to time I still grieve. Once, three years after Carol's death, I was reflecting on the Christian story and realized that one of the sources of my grief was that I was no longer able to love her as I had once done. I can cherish her memory, but she is not physically there to love anymore.

When people die, those who are still alive feel great loss, and a part of that loss is the loss of being able to love those who are gone. This is experienced years later by those who remain alive. Can it also be experienced by the one who is dying, in the moments just before death? If one has lived a life of loving, can one feel the loss of one's self being able to love? As death approaches, can one experience, suddenly and uncontrollably, great grief? Do the dying feel forsaken? Those remaining alive feel forsaken. When Jesus was taken away to be crucified, his followers must have experienced a loss of his love and of their being able to love him in return. Perhaps the agony crying out from the cross is their agony as well.

How is it that the cross was not the end? How does one move from the loss of life and the loss of love to new life and new love? Why didn't the selection pressures against Jesus prevail? Why doesn't the death of a loved one today completely destroy those remaining alive? I think an answer becomes clearer if we set what happens to us in a wider context. We are after all constituted out of our relationships. We are what I have called social-ecological selves — "big selves." When our individual, phenomenal selves become part of a wider context, part of a wider movement, then it is possible that a transformation can take place. The loss of love that accompanies the loss of life can be taken up into ongoing life and a rebirth of love.

When one looks at how Christianity arose out of the death of Jesus, one must recognize that a transformation occurred. One way to understand this transformation is to distinguish between the man Jesus and a wider event we can call the "Christ-event."[5] The Christ event signifies a self that is bigger than the person on the cross. It is all the influences that Jesus had on others while he was still alive, so that when his physical body and brain died, those influences lived on. They coalesced into what Paul called the "mind of Christ" or the "spirit of Christ" — the spirit of undiscriminating love. The Resurrection can be understood as a symbol of this greater reality of a social self that transcends death, of a loving spirit that lives on with a power that eventually becomes at home in the minds of millions of people, growing to become their ideal of what it is to become human.

After Carol's death a series of interactions with others took place that rekindled love in my life. These interactions formed a greater event, so that I felt Carol herself had become transformed, so that she continues to live. It began when I conducted her memorial service. The climax of the service was a letter from me to her, written five months before she finally died — her eulogy. I composed it then and read it to her, and then read it to her again during her final days. At the end of that letter, I said she was taking me on a journey up into high mountains, like the ones we used to enjoy from time to time, hiking together. On the journey into the rough terrain we were supported by many loving people, including some we had come to know only because of her dying. However, in the end it was her and me alone, struggling in the hard climb but also enjoying some remarkable, beautiful views. At the end of the climb, even I could not follow her. She left me to go on, to become transformed into new life, new love.

Yet, in another sense, as I came back down from the mountain heights into the hills and valleys of everyday life, she did not leave me. She became part of a greater event of transformed love in my own life. A few weeks after her memorial service, two friends and I were having lunch. One told me how much he had appreciated the service for Carol and then asked, "Would you be able to conduct a wedding for my daughter?" My reply was, "I am not an ordained minister. Even though I've had the training to be a minister and a M.Div. degree, I never was ordained. Also," I added, "I'm not a justice of the peace or a notary public." His response was, "Why don't you get a notary public's license? My daughter's wedding is in two months."

That is what I did. As I did it, I realized that out of Carol's death new possibilities for me to grow had arisen. They were possibilities that were particularly appropriate, because as I conducted that wedding ceremony, I felt that the spirit of love, which had grown so rich during Carol's dying, was now present for me in this young couple as they took their vows to become husband and wife. In that ceremony I experienced resurrection.

In some of the weddings I have conducted since that first one, I have used New Testament passages about love. I tell of the great, undiscriminating love that the early Christians experienced when they encountered Jesus, a love so powerful, consistent, and extensive that they understood more clearly than ever before that "God is love." I then read from the First Letter of John:

> Beloved, let us love one another, because love is from God; everyone who loves is born of God and knows God. Whoever does not love does not know God for God is love. God's love was revealed among us in this way: God sent his only Son into the world so that we might live through him. In this is love, not that we loved God but that he loved us and sent his Son to be the atoning sacrifice for our sins. Beloved, since God loved us so much, we also ought to love one another. No one has ever seen God; if we love one another, God lives in us, and his love is perfected in us.[6]

When life goes and love fades, new possibilities for life and love arise. The spirit of life and the spirit of love continue as interactions that bring new life in the midst of death and new love in the midst of being forsaken. These creative interactions are the divine to be discerned in the midst of the continual dance of the universe — a dance that includes death as well as life, sorrow as well as joy, suffering as well as wholeness, and the loss and rebirth of love.

✑ Chapter 17 ❧

At Home in the Universe

In our human experience of life interwoven with death, of love interwoven with loss, we come in touch with the dynamic realm of the sacred. Throughout various times and places, humans have had to come to terms with death and loss. It is no different to-day. What is different, however, is a new scientific understanding that places our human living in a much larger universe, a universe that scientific thinking has depersonalized and a universe in which change is fundamental. As one educated in a scientific view of the world, I sometimes feel a sense of homelessness in the vast, imper-sonal, ever changing cosmos. When I face my own life struggles in the face of death, my grief at the loss of love, my expectations for new life and new love, I wonder: Do these have any meaning in the larger scheme of things? What difference does being concerned with human problems of justice make? What difference does being concerned with environmental problems make? Solving such prob-lems, while trying to continue life and love on Earth, seems almost insignificant in the larger scheme of things.

In the last two chapters in this book, I attempt to sketch how we might respond to such problems in a scientific, pluralistic age. How can we regard the vast, impersonal universe in which we live as a home for which we are in part responsible? In addressing issues of size, depersonalization, and change, it may be helpful to compare today's scientific understanding of things with some Christian views. Such a comparison will help us see our problems and their resolution more clearly.

Let's first consider the size of our universe from the perspective of our commonsense experience. We can go outside and observe the universe much as people saw it two thousand years ago at the time of the Roman empire. With our unaided eyes we can see a flat Earth under a dome of heaven. We see the Sun, the Moon, and stars moving across the dome.

When we look at the rivers, lakes, and oceans, we can easily conclude that there are waters that go down beneath the earth; with a little imagination — remember we have no instruments but only our unaided eyesight — we also see waters above the earth from which rains and snows come. We might even come to believe that there is a heaven of heavens beyond the Sun, the Moon, and the stars, beyond the waters above the earth, and that this heaven is the abode of God.

In such a universe of dry land, sun, moon, and stars existing between the waters, it makes cosmological sense to talk about God or messengers of God coming to Earth to speak to humans in dreams or special religious experiences. It even makes sense to say that a divine offspring could come to Earth in human form, die, descend down into the earth to the realm of the dead called Sheol, rise again, ascend back to heaven, and some day in the future come again on the clouds to judge the living and the dead. This is the religiously significant universe constructed out of experience and the cultural thought patterns available to Christians two thousand years ago.[1]

Such a universe may have appeared vast to those inhabiting it, but compared with the universe portrayed by astronomy, it certainly seems compact. Today, based on many controlled observations combined with rational theory, we have mentally constructed another universe. In this universe we live on a spherical planet orbiting an average-sized star. That star is in the suburbs of our Milky Way galaxy of some one hundred billion stars. Our galaxy is just one of some one hundred billion galaxies that are a part of a universe that began expanding some fourteen billion years ago. If we put our fourteen-billion-year universe on a clock of one hour, humanity appears in only the last few seconds.

In terms of astronomical time and space, we have good reason to question the significance of anything that happens on our planet. We have good reason to feel dis-ease, to feel a sense of homelessness in our universe. It is tempting to want to hold on to a more self-contained, cozy universe, as understood by people in ancient times.

Interestingly, some people did not always feel at home in the biblical universe. Looked at in another way, the flat Earth and dome of heaven might remind us of a cave, even of a prison. In early Christianity, people called Gnostics certainly did not feel at home in this universe. The Gnostics believed in the preexistence of the soul and they also believed that they were trapped in a miserable existence on Earth:

> Who flung me into Tibil [this earthly world]? Into Tibil who
> flung me?
> Who cast me into the abode of darkness? . . .
> Why have you snatched me away from my home and brought
> me into this prison, and incarcerated me in this stinking
> body?
> How far are the frontiers of this world of darkness?
> The way we have to go is far and never ending![2]

The Gnostics had a rather pessimistic view of life, to say the least. Their strong dualistic ideas of material evil and spiritual good were declared heresy by the Christian church, because they denied there was any goodness of the world created by God. Yet, the Gnostic feeling of not being at home in this universe has persisted. It is expressed clearly by Thomas à Kempis in his fifteenth-century book *The Imitation of Christ*, one of the most popular books at that time:

> This world is no native country of yours; go where you will,
> you are only a foreigner, only a visitor in it. Nothing will ever
> bring you rest, except being closely united to Jesus.
>   Why stand gaping here? This is no place for you to settle
> down. Heaven is your destination and you should look upon
> this earthly scene only as a transit-camp.[3]

For many — many even today — the relatively compact cosmos of the past is not home.

Let's compare these expressions of alienation with the feelings expressed by Eric Chaisson. After an extended discussion of cosmic evolution and the current scientific picture of the immensities of time and space, he writes:

It is a warmer and friendlier scenario now, many parts of which have become substantiated by experimental science. We are not independent entities, alien to Earth. Earth in turn is not adrift in a vacuum unrelated to the cosmos. The cosmos is no longer cold and hostile because it is our universe. It brought us forth, and it maintains our being. We are, in the very literal sense of the words, children of the universe.[4]

What is behind Chaisson's somewhat homey picture? The main idea is that, in spite of the immensity of the universe, all aspects of it are closely related to us. First, we are made of the stuff of the stars. Second, the very energy that was present as radiation at the beginning of the universe, after many transformations, now courses in our nervous system and drives our feeling and thinking. Third, instead of the billions of years of time being frightening to Chaisson, they reveal to him the toil the universe has undergone to produce us as its offspring. We are the children of much labor, much trial and error, much experimentation and testing through the interaction of natural processes, according to natural laws. This should be somewhat comforting. It should give us some confidence in ourselves — in the "wisdom" of our bodies and in the intellectual capability of our brains to relate appropriately to the rest of nature out of which we have been created.

Some would argue, however, that Chaisson and scientists like him pay a great price as they integrate humanity with the rest of the universe. The picture presented by modern science is of a depersonalized universe. Rather than humanlike agents or even a single divine agent, portrayed in human terms, science presents a universe controlled by nonpersonal forces, processes, and principles interacting with one another. As human persons, how can we feel at home in such a universe? The nonpersonal, naturalistic model of the universe, while it has increased our understanding of things, is a second reason why people do not feel at home in today's universe.

Wasn't the old anthropomorphic picture of many traditional religions much more friendly? For many it probably was and still is. Yet not everyone has seen the universe created and controlled ultimately by personal agents as friendly. Populated by gods and angels, the universe has also been seen as the stage for demons and the devil. Because the personalistic picture of things does not actually alleviate the disintegrating effects of mental disorders, social unrest, disease, and death, some have seen themselves in the midst of a supernatural battlefield — literally caught between the powers of life and death, health and illness, light and darkness, good and evil. The powers of darkness and death have often been portrayed in art in monstrous humanoid images. These powers are intentional agents out to wreak havoc in the world and among human beings. A personalized universe is not necessarily a home.

In contrast, the depersonalized scientific world view may again be friendlier. The nonpersonal, naturalistic picture appears at least more neutral and hence perhaps more benign than that of the personal warfare model. At least the devil is not out to get us. Neither are organisms such as viruses and bacteria. While microorganisms may threaten our health and lives, they do not *intend* to kill us. Rather, following their evolved biological programs, they are simply seeking to continue their existence. Today many people think they can understand and deal more effectively with them in terms of nonpersonal models than in terms of a personalistic ones.

I suggest then that neither the immensity of time and space nor a nonpersonal, naturalistic view of things necessarily leads to thinking and feeling ourselves homeless in the universe. Another problem may be more fundamental — the problem of chance and change.

Today our world is beset with many crises that are calling us to rethink our patterns of living — environmental crises of pollution and climate change; political crises within and between nation-states often fomented by terrorist groups; economic crises of unemployment, inflation, burgeoning national deficits that shift from one part of the globe to another. We also are confronted with positive breakthroughs in science and technology, with exciting new developments in political systems, and with countless new insights as to how to live our lives. Both the crises and the positive breakthroughs, however, are only the symptoms of a more fundamental problem — the continually increasing rate of change and uncertainty in our daily individual and collective lives. In an age of rapid change and much uncertainty, how can we find for ourselves a meaningful place in the scheme of things? How can we be at home in the universe?

The picture of cosmic, biological, and cultural evolution from the sciences supports our experience of change. Moreover, the scientific picture also suggests that we should not be surprised at uncertainty, because from an evolutionary perspective most change is brought about by chance — the chance interaction of different causal sequences of events. These chance interactions of causal chains constantly disrupt our lives, sometimes for good and sometimes for ill — but the problem is that the disruption is usually unpredictable.

Take our individual lives as examples. They are constantly subject to chance and change. Think what happens to a well-planned day. If you are like me, you try to have a plan for your day when you get up in the morning. Often our plans are disrupted time and again in unexpected ways in our interactions with others. What are these other people trying to do? They are simply trying to carry out their own daily plans. Living with others means continuously having to adapt to the unexpected that causally affects our lives and at times even our destinies.

What applies to us on a daily basis also applies in our lifetimes — the unexpected falling in love, getting pregnant, birthing a child with genetic defects, having a heart attack in middle age, discovering cells growing out of control in our bodies. How often have our lives been changed by the unexpected? The same is true for societies and, according to Darwinian theory, for species. Different sequences of events collide with one another randomly, unpredictably, in our individual, societal, and biological lives. What meaning can we find in such a world of chance and necessity? How can we dance to the music of the spheres if the tune is constantly changing?

This problem of change by chance may underlie the other two problems we have discussed. Change may be responsible for the ancient feeling of homelessness, even in a relatively compact universe. It also may contribute in part to the desire of many people to see the ultimate source of existence as a personal supreme being.

Why did some ancients view the flat Earth under the dome of heaven not as a cozy home but as a cavelike prison? One reason seems to have been the impermanence and randomness of life on Earth. Almost twenty-five hundred years ago, Plato and his followers concluded that even though this world might appear real to our senses, the transience of things and the vicissitudes of "fickle fate" indicated this world was only a reflection, a second class reality. For the Platonists, for the more radical Gnostics, for the medieval Christians dealing with the same problem and influenced by Platonism, the true reality was not this cavelike world of appearance and change, of "puppets casting shadows on a wall," but the realm of ideal, permanent forms. By abandoning the world of change and by climbing the ladder of intellectual and spiritual discipline, one could come into contact with the realm of eternal forms — the eternally true, good, and beautiful. Here some, following Plato, found order and meaning.

Some Christian theologians took over the Platonic eternal forms and called them the "mind of God." In doing this they regarded God as analogous to the human person and human mind. It is important to recognize that the view of God as person is an attempt to express the idea that there is an underlying order of things and that change in the world is not due to chance but is part of a divine plan. In keeping, Christians have not attributed to the ultimate creative reality conceived as person all the characteristics of humanity, especially not those characteristics that have negative consequences. The view of God as person has been the view that a rational mind transcends the world of change and that human beings can find meaning for their lives, can find an eternal home, in the blissful contemplation of the mind of God. Thus, one might see the traditional Christian idea of heaven and the personal view of God as ways of responding to the human quest for order and meaning.

Modern science is also engaged in this quest. However, science does not seek order and meaning beyond the world of space and time in Platonic eternal forms, or in heaven and the mind of God. Instead it seeks order and meaning in this world as it searches for the laws of the universe, of human society, and of individual biopsychological life. Science too seeks order and stability in the midst of chance and change. It also seeks a home in the universe.

Science discovers that there are laws, that there is order in the universe. If we use a musical metaphor, we might say science is discovering the "beat" of the universe; it uncovers the underlying rhythms of nature. Science also discovers something else besides the underlying rhythms. It discovers that the tune is constantly changing. Discovering the laws of nature does not eliminate chance and change, because lawful sequences of events still affect each other in unpredictable ways. The ideas of nonequilibrium thermodynamics, the Darwinian theory of random variation and natural selection, and the need to use statistical analysis in the social sciences — all illustrate this point. The universe is not completely orderly. It has much order, but it also is the scene of what appears to be much improvisation in a constant search for new melodies.

A good musical analogy for what science is telling us is that the dynamic universe in which we live is like jazz. I know this sounds strange, but think about it for a minute. In jazz the drums, bass, guitar, and sometimes piano provide the basic rhythm or beat. The front line instruments — trumpet, trombone, and clarinet — continually improvise on the tune by interacting with one another and thus creating new variations on the melody. Let's think about this in relation to the universe. Not just the music of the spheres but the jazz music of the spheres! The underlying laws of nature supply the rhythm, and the constant chance interaction of causal sequences of events improvises new genetic, behavioral, and intellectual melodies in various environments. Such a universe seems to be our home. Can we see and feel ourselves at home in it?[5]

I think we can. Here are three things that will help us use chance creatively rather than letting it completely disorganize and destroy us. Perhaps you can think of some more. First, we can use our intelligence, our brains that have been created in the fourteen billion years of evolution, to anticipate when we might be confronted with an increased rate of possible chance events. We often do this in our daily lives. For example, under certain traffic conditions such as rain-surfaced streets or rush hour traffic, when the possibility of chance encounters with other cars increases, we become more alert and drive defensively. Similarly, as we travel through life we can be more attentive to the rate of chance occurrences in "high density" situations. When our lives become busier and more complicated, we can be more alert to the possibility of chance encounters. We also can follow the practice of many religious leaders and contemporary psychologists and reduce the stress of chance by turning to the stability of simpler living, of solitude and silence, and of contemplative prayer and meditation. We can reenter our core selves, our sacred centers.

Second, we can place ourselves in communities of supporting persons. Families, friends, colleagues at work, and members of religious communities can be sources of support. We can support one another when chance encounters with such things as microorganisms or foreign ideas invade our bodies and brains to disrupt our physical and mental equilibrium. We can never fully anticipate physical illness or mental unrest, and both of these can range from the equivalent of a cold to life-threatening and even death-dealing blows to our orderly lives. Yet, in caring communities of people, who accept us as we are and give us their support, we can find help when the improvisations of nature and society threaten to overwhelm us.

Finally, we can use the chance encounters of life as opportunities to participate in the jazz of creative existence. Creation itself occurs through unforeseen, chance recombinations of events. Once we understand this, we can be at home in the universe, uniting ourselves with the processes that have brought us into being by joining the improvisational music of the spheres.

Let me offer as an example a situation that is not uncommon but from which I have learned a great deal. A fourteen-year-old boy's mother dies after an extended illness. The boy is left alone with his father, who fortunately proves to be good at responding to tragedy creatively, at adapting and improvising a new life, much the way a jazz trumpeter might improvise a new melody. Thus their life together is good, even though the loss of the mother and wife is felt deeply. Then the father plays still another tune; he remarries and brings himself and his son a wonderful new wife and mother and a new, large, and charming array of aunts, uncles, and cousins. More than half a century later I am still benefiting from the new relationships. I'll always be thankful that my father was a good improviser, that he responded creatively to chance events that in one sense were quite destructive. Dad was not a musician in the ordinary sense of the word. But when it came to dealing creatively with chance events, he was an excellent front line player of the jazz of life.

One trick of living, I suggest, is not only to try to control the rate of change in our lives, not only to support one another in times of need. It is also to welcome chance — to welcome the causal sequences of events that impinge unexpectedly on our lives — as giving us opportunities for growth. Even as we live our lives on Earth here and now, we can join the music of the spheres. We can learn to follow the fundamental rhythms, the laws of nature, in the dance of life. And in keeping with the rhythm or beat we can continually improvise new patterns of living. In doing so we join the rest of the universe in the ongoing process of dynamic creation. We come to feel at home in an evolving universe.

✔ Chapter 18 ✔

Earth: A Child of God

We are living in a scientific, pluralistic age. In an age of diverse cultures, of scientific knowledge and technology, we have been exploring how we can be related to the divine, as it is present in our midst. We are exploring the possibility that the sacred is the process of ongoing creation in the world, the dance of ever evolving nature. The divine destabilizing *spirit* and restructuring *word* constantly call us to become fresh and new. They call us *in* the midst of, *through* the midst of death, loss, and suffering. Our harmony with God is a harmony involving the most difficult transformations of self and our relationships with one another and the world.

We have recognized that our scientific technology and narrow personal and social self-interest are putting our planet in peril. Our biologically evolved natures and our culturally evolved practices, products of earlier divine creativity, have not equipped us to deal with the vast power science gives us. We are called once again to reestablish ourselves in harmony with nature. We need to see our kinship with other creatures. We need to see ourselves as webs of cosmos, life, and culture, so that we and the rest of our planet can continue and flourish.

Our human living must be set in the context of a much larger life, that of the universe. Even though we are descended from the rest of nature, our minds can barely grasp the immense size of our universe. In this vast universe creation, destruction, and re-creation occur at magnitudes we can barely fathom. Our daily experience of loss and death pales in comparison with mass extinctions that destroyed countless species only to prepare the way for our own. Could catastrophes such as the chance collision of an asteroid with the earth sixty-six million years ago — which ended the era of the dinosaurs — occur again to end the era of *Homo sapiens?* Such events are possible. How can we understand our local union with the divine creativity that brings greater good for ourselves and our planet when on a larger scale of things that same creativity may destroy all our efforts — only to produce new, unforeseen, nonhuman good?

In an attempt to respond to this question I would like to engage in a thought experiment. The origins of this thought experiment are in a class I have taught that compares the scientific portrait of evolution with creation stories from a variety of cultures around the world. In this comparison I have been struck with how the evolutionary scenario is like many of the emergence myths from traditional societies. These myths depict a birth process. Humans emerge from the earth, the world is born from divine parents, everything grows from a seed, or all is generated out of a cosmic egg.[1]

My thought experiment is not a scientific one. It is one of religious conceptualization in an age of science. It is an attempt to suggest a metaphor that I think encompasses all the concerns I have raised above as part of a single cosmic journey. The journey is one of being born. The metaphor is that the earth is a child of God and we humans are the developing mind of the earth, with the power to shape its destiny, which includes our own destiny.

Metaphors are widely used in both science and religion. They try to capture significant elements of something not fully understood with an idea that is more familiar. The Confucian idea that heaven and Earth are our parents, the Hebrew notion that Yahweh is king of the universe, and the Christian notion that Christ is the light of the world are all metaphors. So is the scientific idea that the universe began as a big bang. None of these metaphors is to be taken literally. While metaphors show similarities between things being compared, unpacking the metaphors also uncovers differences. As Sallie McFague has put it, a metaphor indicates that " 'this' is like 'that' but ... it is also *not* like 'that.' "[2] Metaphors, therefore, are not to be taken literally. They are not to be pushed too far. However, they are serious attempts to extend our grasp of things from our familiar world into the unfamiliar.

The metaphor I am suggesting is that the entire evolving universe is like a birth process that gives rise to children. One such child is our planet Earth, which has become alive with the advent of life and has become self-conscious with the advent of the human mind. The human mind is the self-reflective thinking layer of the earth, what Pierre Teilhard de Chardin called the noosphere.[3]

In today's scientific, pluralistic age, a metaphor in a religious thought experiment must be credible in the light of scientific understandings. It also must be open to a variety of theological interpretations so that it can be used in a variety of religious communities. Finally, the metaphor must involve us personally, giving direction and motivation to the way we live our lives. All this is a big order, but meeting these requirements is necessary if a metaphor and its narrative development in story are to have motivational power for sufficiently large numbers of people in today's world.

I think this metaphor that the earth is a child of an evolving universe is scientifically credible. It fits the general picture of cosmic, biological, and cultural evolution portrayed by science. It also suggests some things that scientists may want to take into account — general hypotheses implied by the metaphor. First, the birth metaphor suggests that we view the evolution of the universe as a coherent single event with many subevents along the way. Second, a birth event, though coherent and lawlike, involves random interactions. Gene recombinations and influences on the fetal environment can affect the outcome of the birth process in unpredictable ways, ways that are not always good from the perspective of parents. The coherence of the event might relate to the insights of scientists who interpret all the fine tunings in nature as part of an inherent design that gives rise to humans (a version of the anthropic principle). The unpredictability of outcomes relates to the thinking of those scientists who see the evolution of the earth and all that it contains, including us, as owing to chance as well as law.[4]

In religious terms, we might say the entire Earth, including humanity, is a child of God, and God is that which gives birth to such children. Such a God may be conceived in a variety of ways. Following Sallie McFague, one might think of God as a transcendent-immanent divine mother — more than but including the universe as God's body.[5] Following the thinking of Gordon

Kaufman, one might construct a concept of God as serendipitous creativity, a unifying symbol for the set of conditions of nature and history that has given rise to the earth and its self-conscious thinking layer.[6] Many theological and philosophical positions could make use of the metaphor that the evolution of the universe is a birth process that gives rise to the whole earth, including humanity, as an offspring of that process.

If the earth-child metaphor can be used in the context of a variety of theologies, and if it is consistent with contemporary science, there is still the question of whether it provides motivational power. Can it help us respond to the challenges to living we have raised in this book, so that we will behave in ways that show greater care for our planet and all its inhabitants? Embodied in the following metaphorical narrative of the birth of the earth-child is a loosely structured argument intended to suggest that humans can flourish in a way that cherishes the earth and all its inhabitants, even though we are just a small speck in a vast evolving universe and even though forces beyond our control may bring all our efforts to nought.[7]

Although it may not be necessary, it helps me to view the evolving universe as the birth of an earth-child if I imagine myself in a different time frame. As humans we measure time in terms of the daily rotation of our planet, the periods of the Moon, our planet's circling of the Sun, and the human life cycle. In our human time frame a birth takes nine months, and it takes between one and two decades for most human beings to become self-conscious and responsible. In such a time frame, a birth process that takes billions of years seems almost inconceivable, even ridiculous. However, if we imagine a butterfly and measure time in terms of the butterfly life cycle, the human life cycle would seem immense. I suggest that we think of our human time frame in relation to the history of the universe in roughly the same proportion that we might think of a butterfly time frame in relation to the human. We might do this by regarding a billion years in the human time frame as a year in a cosmic time frame. In "fourteen years" the divine creativity inherent in the universe gives birth to the earth and the earth-child begins to grow. There is precedent for this in religious thought, both in the East and the West. When the Hindu deity Brahma breathes out the universe and then inhales all back into itself, billions of human years pass. "A thousand ages in thy sight are but an evening gone" is a statement of Psalm 90, echoed in one Christian hymn.

If we alter our time frame to take such a cosmic perspective, a narrative of the evolution of the universe might go something like this. Out of a singularity (like a single cell or seed) the universe inflates. The seed of energy expands, cools, and begins to differentiate itself into subatomic particles. In the first few "days," some of these coagulate into hydrogen and helium atoms. As "weeks" go by, and under the impulse of the cosmic "wind," fluctuations occur in the particles of matter, uniting some of them together in huge, proto-galactic clouds. Within the clouds, fluctuations again occur to catalyze the formation of pockets of hydrogen and helium atoms. Under the laws of gravity, these collect more atoms, until by swirling centrifugal forces and gravitational contractions a density of enough atoms is reached. Ignition — stars are formed in the galactic clouds.

Like cells in a growing body, stars are not permanent. They go through their main sequence of nuclear fusion until all their hydrogen is fused to helium. Smaller stars die. Larger stars, much more massive than our Sun, expand and contract, heat up, and begin fusing helium. They expand and contract more, until in a massive contraction under gravitational forces they rebound in spectacular explosions with temperatures high enough to create all the heavier elements.

After such birth throes, the cosmic equivalent to a mother's labor, news stars are born. One, our Sun, has a planet, an earth-child. Over the coming "months," nourished by radiation from the Sun, the earth-child grows. Self-replicating molecules are created. Cells are born. Sexual reproduction arises. Species differentiate and evolve.

Through its growth and development, major changes occur in the body of the earth-child. Ninety-nine percent of the species that help form the living tissue of the body die off, only to be replaced by others as new life tissue. Some die in major catastrophes — mass extinctions — occasioned by the dynamics of the evolving planet or by extra-planetary events such as asteroid collisions. Through such events, even because of them, the earth-child has grown to an estimated ten million species of life woven together as tissues of the earth body.

Near the end of the first five "years" of earth-child development, a thinking layer begins to take shape. Higher primates and then humans are created. At first they are like small collections of cells, spreading out from Africa over the planet. With large brains relative to their physical size, cells of humanity invent languages and begin to wonder about their own origins. Cultural myths are developed to explain the universe, moral codes to promote social bonding, rituals to help encode the emerging wisdom for life and practice into future generations of brains. Recently the earth-child has grown to unite many smaller collections of brains in large-scale civilizations. Most recently the brain of the earth-child has begun, through science, to understand its own origins, even though it still dimly grasps it own place and purpose in the overall scheme of things.

In this way we have been born, as Robert Weston puts it, out of the stars. Out of the stars have we come, in the cradle of time and space. The earth-child is born and is now growing in life and thought. Can it also grow in love? Can its thinking layer come to love the rest of itself, the entire earth as a child of God?

In terms of our cosmic time frame, perhaps we are reaching a stage of adolescence. There is much ahead of the earth-child and its human mind, though we but dimly perceive it. However, we need to grow beyond childhood. What happens in the future in the earth-child's mind will make a significant difference.

There are a number of implications of this narrative of the earth-child for the relation between humanity and the rest of the earth, and for how we are to understand our place in the scheme of things. First, we must emphasize that in the narrative the child is the entire earth with humans as its reflective mind, its self-consciousness. Like all children, the entire earth-child is precious. It has great intrinsic value, just as an entire human child has intrinsic value. Further, just as our human bodies do a lot on their own, give rise to our minds, and are vital for our continued mental functioning, so the earth does much on its own, gives rise to sentience in many species and to self-reflection with language in humanity, and is vital for the continuation of its sphere of mind. Yet the self-conscious mind of the earth, humanity, can for better or worse, with ever increasing knowledge but still with considerable ignorance, steer the course of the earth. It can steer this child of God toward self-deterioration, impoverishing the child, or it can help the earth-body of the child to continue to flourish and support the earth-mind, the human-civilization aspect of the child.

It seems to me that the earth-child is only now becoming self-conscious in humanity, and that this self-consciousness is still acting childlike, demanding to be taken care of by that which has created the earth-child. We expect that all our needs will be met and that all we have to do is demand. We are approaching adolescence. We are not clear what to do with our mental power that allows us to control information and energy-matter and thereby radically affect the future course of events. We sometimes wildly try new experiments in living without much foresight. However, with the rise of global environmental problems, it is beginning to dawn in part of the earth's reflective mind that we are not thinking and acting in a way that contributes to the long-term well-being of the body of the earth-child.

What then is the place of humanity in the scheme of things? In terms of the narrative, what can be expected of us? Perhaps it is as simple as "growing up" — becoming a responsible self-consciousness of the earth. It is to find ways to act in concert with our body — with the rest of the earth and its wisdom — to evolve an earth civilization in harmony with the rest of the planet that can continue to flourish for a long time to come. Such an "earth adult" could also reach out to contact other planets connected to other stars, other children of God.

What about the uncertainty of the future? What about that which is beyond our control? What about the threat of a chance mass extinction destroying much of the earth-child, perhaps even destroying its self-consciousness? For one thing, mass extinctions unleash new potentials. Maybe there is more to the birth of this child of God than we know. Maybe we are not the full flourishing of the child. Yet, if we are, then we must recognize that not all children reach maturity. Sometimes forces beyond our control take away our human children; and extraterrestrial forces may also adversely affect or even destroy the earth-child.

We also know that human children, when they reach adolescence, may do things that lead to their own self-destruction. This is often due in large part to what goes on in their minds. Even self-conscious adult humans can get caught in habits and addictive ways of living that are self-destructive of mind and body alike.

Yet adolescents usually want to become a healthy adults, live long lives, and be able to develop their potentials creatively. I think this can also be true of the mind of the earth-child. As human beings become aware of the long history of evolutionary processes that have created the earth-child, they might begin to glimpse some of its future possibilities. These include a healthy planet rich in flourishing biodiversity and a human civilization where the basic maintenance needs of all are met and where all have the opportunity to develop their potentials for nonmaterial achievements of peace, friendship, beauty, love, and wisdom.

Is the glimpse of such a future for the earth-child enough to help motivate us human beings to move beyond narrow-minded, short-term, material self-satisfaction? I do not know. It is not easy to leave selfish ways behind, to move beyond the childhood of our biological and cultural conditioning into responsible adulthood. Yet, when I think that I am a "big self," that what I do in my life influences how I live on in the future, I feel a sense of responsibility for the wider web of life of which I am a part. When I think about what gives my life quality, I realize that friendship and love are much more fulfilling than material goods. When I feel the transforming power of the creative process and the excitement that comes from participating in the emergence of new ways of thinking and living, I realize that continuing to dance with the sacred is truly to flourish as a human being.

As part of the earth-child, we are all heirs of the sacred creative dance that has been going on for fourteen billion years, giving birth to the earth-child. We are part of the promise of the future as we help to create an earth-adult though continuing to dance with the sacred. Our planet Earth, including our human species, was born out of billions of years of cosmic evolution. In the emerging global village we can see ourselves as part of the gathering of the consciousness of the planet. As we understand the divine dynamics at the heart of the birth process, we can recognize that we are part of a sacred creativity that is still bringing the earth-child to fruition. Seeing the plurality of cultures and the rise of modern science as parts of the developing consciousness of the earth, we can appreciatively remember and use the wisdom that humanity has already accumulated for living in harmony with its own earth-body. Having experienced transforming creativity that deepens and widens our love, we can love all the earth and its inhabitants even as we love our social-ecological human selves. In loving the earth, we love the web of life in us and of which we are a part.

Earth — a child of God, born in the sacred dance of spirit and word, random fluctuations and inherent laws. Humans — the evolved mind of the earth-child. As each of us, a part of the earth-mind, continues to grow through creative transformation in knowledge and love, the planet that is our home in the universe will also continue to grow and flourish.

Notes

1: Thinking about God in a New Way

1. Charles Sanders Peirce, "How to Make Our Ideas Clear," in *Collected Papers,* ed. Charles Hartshorne and Paul Weiss (Cambridge, Mass.: Harvard University Press, Belknap Press, 1965), 5:248–71.

2. Two of Wieman's many writings that are good introductions to his thought are Henry Nelson Wieman, *The Source of Human Good* (Carbondale, Ill.: Southern Illinois University Press, 1946) and *Man's Ultimate Commitment* (Carbondale, Ill.: Southern Illinois University Press, 1958).

3. Karl E. Peters, "The Concept of God and the Method of Science: An Exploration of the Possibility of Scientific Theology" (Ph.D. diss., Columbia University [Ann Arbor, Mich.: University Microfilms, 1971]).

4. Many of Burhoe's writings are in various issues of *Zygon: Journal of Religion and Science.* A useful collection is Ralph Wendell Burhoe, *Toward a Scientific Theology* (Belfast: Christian Journals Limited, 1981). A helpful intellectual biography is David R. Breed, *Yoking Science and Religion: The Life and Thought of Ralph Wendell Burhoe* (Chicago: Zygon Books, 1992).

5. Robert T. Weston, "Out of the Stars," in *Singing the Living Tradition* (Boston: Beacon Press, 1993), no. 530.

2: Science and Societies in the Emerging Global Village

1. Using a new method for analyzing the background radiation left over from the big bang, some scientists now calculate that the universe is fourteen billion years old. This calculation is accurate to within half a billion years. R. Cowen, "Age of the Universe: A New Determination," *Science News* 160 (October 27, 2001): 261.

2. Gen 1:4, 10, 12, 18, 21, 25, 31.

3. In the last part of this book, I will develop the theme that, in an evolving universe, new creation always involves destruction, that new life involves loss and death. Here I am talking about destruction, loss, and death that needlessly diminishes creativity in human civilization and on our planet.

4. Deut 30:19.

3: Peril in the Global Village

1. Eric Chaisson, *Cosmic Dawn: The Origins of Matter and Life* (New York: W. W. Norton, 1981).

2. Jessica Tuchman Matthews, interview by Bill Moyers, *World of Ideas* videocassette, WNET, New York and WTTW, Chicago, 1989.

3. George Edgin Pugh's groundbreaking *The Biological Origin of Human Values* (New York: Basic Books, 1977), 173–337 gives a helpful analysis of the kinds of biological motivators resulting from evolution. He divides them into motivators for self-preservation, social cooperation, and intellectual inquiry. For a summary of his thinking, see George Edgin Pugh, "Values and the Theory of Motivation," *Zygon: Journal of Religion and Science* 14 (March 1979): 53–82.

4. Richard Dawkins, *The Selfish Gene* (Oxford: Oxford University Press, 1976); Donald T. Campbell, "On the Conflicts between Biological and Social Evolution and between Psychology and Moral Tradition," *American Psychologist* 30 (December 1975): 1103–126, reprinted in *Zygon: Journal of Religion and Science* 11 (September 1976): 167–208; Ralph Wendell Burhoe, "The Source of Civilization in the Natural Selection of Coadapted Information in Genes and Culture," and "Religion's Role in Human Evolution: The Missing Link between Ape-Man's Selfish Genes and Civilized Altruism," in *Toward a Scientific Theology* (Belfast: Christian Journals Limited, 1981), 151–233.

5. Relational thinking in feminist psychology, philosophy, and theology is beginning to present a different view of what is good for humans. Value is to be found in relationships, not in isolated, individual, self-development. I will be developing some similar ideas in later chapters.

6. "How the Dinosaurs Died," *Science Impact* (May 1989): 3–4.

7. David Raup, *Extinction: Bad Genes or Bad Luck?* (New York: W. W. Norton, 1991).

4: Sacred Centers

1. *Spirit and Nature: The Moyers Collection*, videocassette (Princeton, N.J.: Film for the Humanities & Sciences, 1997).

2. John Fenton in *Religions of Asia* develops a three-part model for the cross-cultural study of the world's religions. The first part of the model is that religions develop relationships between human beings and sacred realities in response to basic human needs. I have been illustrating this part with the example of Audrey Shenandoah. The second part of the model is that religions satisfy fundamental human needs through a process of transformation. The third part is that religions communicate their understandings of sacred realities and processes of transformation from one generation to the next with the aid of symbols. John Fenton et al., *Religions of Asia*, 3rd ed. (New York: St. Martin's Press, 1993), 4–16.

3. Ward H. Goodenough, "Self-Maintenance as a Religious Concern," *Zygon: Journal of Religion and Science* 23 (June 1988): 117–28, esp. 119–20.

4. Fenton et al., *Religions of Asia*, 34.

5. See Ilya Prigogine, *From Being to Becoming: Time and Complexity in the Physical Sciences* (San Francisco: W. H. Freeman, 1980); Prigogine, "The Rediscovery of Time," *Zygon: Journal of Religion and Science* 19 (December 1984): 443–47; and Arthur Peacocke, "Thermodynamics and Life," *Zygon: Journal of Religion and Science* 19 (December 1984): 395–432.

6. Kent Danner, ed. *The American Wilderness in the Words of John Muir* (Waukesha, Wis.: Country Beautiful, 1973), 58.

7. Arthur Peacocke, "Chance and the Life Game," *Zygon: Journal of Religion and Science* 14 (December 1979): 316. This entire essay offers an excellent summary of thermodynamics in creation with a helpful philosophical and theological interpretation.

8. John Hick, *God Has Many Names* (Louisville, Ky.: Westminster, 1982), 7.

5: Creative Mystery

1. William Theodore de Bary, Wing-tsit Chan, and Burton Watson, comps., *Sources of Chinese Tradition*, vol. 1 (New York: Columbia University Press, 1960), 51.

2. Ralph T. H. Griffith, trans., *The Hymns of the Rig Veda* (Benares: E. J. Lazarus and Co., 1896), no. 129, Book 10. Quoted in David S. Noss and John B. Noss, *A History of the World's Religions*, 9th ed. (New York: Macmillan, 1994), 95.

3. Nikos Kazantzakis, *Report to Greco* (New York: Simon and Schuster, 1965), 291–92. Quoted in John B. Cobb Jr., *God and the World* (Philadelphia: Westminster, 1976), 53.

4. Noss and Noss, *A History of the World's Religions*, 14.

5. Gordon D. Kaufman, *God, Mystery, Diversity: Christian Theology in a Pluralistic World* (Minneapolis: Fortress Press, 1996), 101–9.

6. Ibid., 109.

7. James Watson, *The Double Helix: A Personal Account of the Discovery of the Structure of DNA* (New York: Penguin Putnam, New American Library, 1991).

8. Gordon D. Kaufman, *Theology for a Nuclear Age* (Philadelphia: Westminster Press, 1985), 40.

9. Ibid., 40–41.

6: To Err Is Divine

1. This point is nicely illustrated by the children's book by Charlotte Foltz Jones and John O'Brien, *Mistakes That Worked* (New York: Doubleday, 1994).

2. J. Bronowski, "New Concepts in the Evolution of Complexity: Stratified Stability and Unbounded Plans," *Zygon: Journal of Religion and Science* 5 (March 1970): 24.

3. Albert Einstein, *Relativity: The Special and General Theory* (New York: Crown, 1961).

4. Steve Phelan, professor of English, said this in one of our meetings with a student as we supervised her independent study on creativity.

5. Carl Sandburg, "Nocturne in a Deserted Brickyard," in *American Poetry and Prose*, ed. Norman Foerster (Boston: Houghton Mifflin, 1952), 750.

6. Mark 2:27.

7. Mark 2:17.

8. Mark 14:36. The intimacy of this term is emphasized in its location in the Gospels. Jesus uses it in his prayer in Gethsemane. It might be said that at this time he was closest to God as he asked God to take away the bitter cup of suffering and death.

7: Darwin and the Dance of Tao

1. Lao Tsu, *Tao Te Ching*, trans. Gia-Fu Feng and Jane English (Random House, Vintage Books, 1972), no. 78.

2. Denise L. Carmody and John T. Carmody, *Christianity: An Introduction* (Belmont, Calif.: Wadsworth, 1983), 20.

3. Matthew Arnold, "Calm Soul of All Things," in *Singing the Living Tradition* (Boston: Beacon Press, 1993), no. 88.

8: Divine Dynamics: Spirit and Word

A longer and more complex version of this chapter was published as "Toward a Physics, Metaphysics, and Theology of Creation: A Trinitarian View," *Religion, Science, and Public Policy*, ed. Frank T. Birtel (New York: Crossroad, 1987), 96–102.

1. Prigogine, *From Being to Becoming: Time and Complexity in the Physical Sciences* (San Francisco: W. H. Freeman, 1980).

2. A. Katchalsky, "Thermodynamics of Flow and Biological Organization," *Zygon: Journal of Religion and Science* (June 1971): 104–7.

3. Prigogine, *From Being to Becoming*, 126.

4. Joan Centrella, quoted in *Science 83*, 4 (December): 8.

5. Eric Chaisson, "Cosmic Evolution: A Synthesis of Matter and Life," *Zygon: Journal of Religion and Science* 14 (March 1979): 27.

6. Ibid., 28.

7. Ibid.

8. Prigogine, *From Being to Becoming*, 126–28. The material from Ramon Margalef is found in E. Margalef, *Seminaire D'ecologie Quantitative* (Venice: third session of E4, 1976).

9. Since I initially wrote this section on nonequilibrium thermodynamics and creation, others have called my attention to similarities with chaos theory. Chaos theory also sees creation occurring through unpredictable variations that give rise to new order in a universe in which everything is interconnected. Ian Barbour gives a good, brief summary of both nonequilibrium thermodynamics and chaos theory in *Religion and Science: Historical and Contemporary Issues* (San Francisco: Harper San Francisco, 1997), 181–84. Chaos theory, nonequilibrium thermodynamics, and evolution — combined with computer and information science — inform the original and thought provoking philosophical theology of

James E. Huchingson in *Pandemonium Tremendum: Chaos and Mystery in the Life of God* (Cleveland: Pilgrim Press, 2001).

10. Jeffrey Wicken has developed one such correlation with an understanding of creation from ancient Hinduism. He draws a parallel between the notion of the creator deity Brahma breathing out the universe and the dissipation of energy from states of potential work to states of thermodynamic equilibrium via the creation of structures organized in the manner described in this reflection, following the work of Prigogine. Jeffrey S. Wicken, "The Cosmic Breath: Reflections on the Thermodynamics of Creation," *Zygon: Journal of Religion and Science* 19 (December 1984): 487–505.

11. "Spirit," *The Hastings Encyclopedia of Religion and Ethics* (New York: Charles Scribner and Sons, 1925).

12. See John 1:1.

9: Our Natural Family

1. Rom 7:15.

2. A readable account of the biological bases for human morality and immorality is by science writer Robert Wright, *The Moral Animal, Why We Are the Way We Are: The New Science of Evolutionary Psychology* (New York: Random House, Vintage Books, 1994). Chapter 7, "Families," is on kin altruism, and chapter 9, "Friends," is on reciprocal altruism.

3. See Solomon H. Katz, "An Evolutionary Concept of Cuisine," *Human Nature* 1 (1999): 246, 249.

4. Eikeen Kaibara, "Precepts for Children," in *Sources of Japanese Tradition*, ed. R. Tsunoda et al. (New York: Columbia University Press, 1958), 367–68.

5. Eric J. Chaisson, "Cosmic Evolution: A Synthesis of Matter and Life," *Zygon: Journal of Religion and Science* 14 (March 1979): 39.

6. Philip Hefner, "Nature, God's Great Project," *Zygon: Journal of Religion and Science* 27 (September 1992): 330–31.

7. What follows is based on Holmes Rolston's discussions of the intrinsic value of individual organisms and of species, and the systemic value of ecosystems. The way I develop his thought in the following line of reasoning is an attempt to simplify his careful, extensive discussion. See Holmes Rolston III, *Environmental Ethics: Duties to and Values in the Natural World* (Philadelphia: Temple University Press, 1988), esp. 97–119, 146–58, 186–201.

8. Ursula Goodenough, *The Sacred Depths of Nature* (New York: Oxford University Press, 1998), 33–45.

9. See Frans de Waal, *Good Natured: The Origins of Right and Wrong in Humans and Other Animals* (Cambridge, Mass.: Harvard University Press, 1996).

10. Rolston, *Environmental Ethics*, 145.

10: Our Social-Ecological Selves

1. An earlier version of this and the next chapter has been published as Karl E. Peters, "A Social-Ecological Understanding of the Human Self," *Religious*

Humanism (Winter 1992): 9–25. These chapters are based on Ralph Wendell Burhoe, "The Concepts of God and Soul in a Scientific View of Human Purpose," in *Toward a Scientific Theology* (Belfast: Christian Journals Limited, 1981), 112–50. Suggesting that the soul is whatever continues as the real core of a human being, Burhoe writes: "The real core of human nature is not any particular body but an enduring pattern of flow. The flow pattern is generated by the interaction of the energy and boundary conditions set by habitat (or cosmotype), genotype, and culturetype, resulting in unending successions of ever-evolving levels of living forms" (140). My thinking in this chapter is an attempt to explain the meaning of this passage.

2. Philip Hefner, *The Human Factor: Evolution, Culture, and Religion* (Minneapolis: Fortress Press, 1993), 29. For a proposed scientific model of biocultural evolution that underlies the position developed here, see ibid., 198. The model was developed by biological anthropologist Solomon H. Katz, "Exploring the Model of Biocultural Evolution" (paper delivered at the 159th National Meeting of the American Association for the Advancement of Science, Boston, February 15, 1993).

11: Morality and Meaning for Our "Big Selves"

1. Max Rudolf Lemberg, "The Complementarity of Religion and Science: A Trialogue," *Zygon: Journal of Religion and Science* 14 (December 1979): 373–74.
2. Matt. 25:14–30.
3. Huston Smith, *The World's Religions* (San Francisco: HarperSanFrancisco, 1991), 287–88.

12: The Development of the Earth and Quality of Life

An earlier version of this chapter appeared in the journal *Religious Humanism* (Summer 1976), 134–38.

1. Robert Heilbroner, *An Inquiry into the Human Prospect* (New York: W. W. Norton, 1974), 13–27.
2. Daniel R. DeNicola, "A Typology of Conceptions of the Good," *The Personalist* (January 1978): 38–46.

13: Seeking Our Sacred Center

1. Gal. 5:19–23.
2. Robert Wright, *The Moral Animal, Why We Are the Way We Are: The New Science of Evolutionary Psychology* (New York: Random House, Vintage Books, 1994).
3. Richard Wrangham and Dale Peterson, *Demonic Males: Apes and the Origins of Human Violence* (Boston: Houghton Mifflin, 1996).
4. Frans de Waal, *Good Natured: The Origins of Right and Wrong in Humans and Other Animals* (Cambridge, Mass.: Harvard University Press, 1996).

5. Paul MacLean, *The Triune Brain in Evolution: Role of Paleocerebral Functions* (New York: Plenum Press, 1990).

6. Victor S. Johnston, *Why We Feel: The Science of Human Emotions* (Reading, Mass.: Perseus Books, 1999), 109–12.

7. Ibid., 91.

8. Richard C. Schwartz, *Internal Family Systems Therapy* (New York: Guilford Press, 1995), especially the chapter on "Viewing Individuals as Systems," 27–60. The description of our inner ecology in this and the following paragraphs is based largely on a summary by Marjorie Hall Davis, "One Thing Needful," a sermon at the First Congregational Church of Granby, Conn., February 27, 2000.

9. Schwartz, *Internal Family Systems Therapy*, 36–41.

10. Antonio Damasio, *The Feeling of What Happens: Body and Emotion in the Making of Consciousness* (New York: Harcourt Brace & Company, 1999). For summary charts of the three selves, see pp. 174–75 and 199. Specific regions of the brain are related to each of the three selves. Some brain regions involved in the proto-self are brain stem nuclei, the hypothalamus, the insular cortex, the cortices known as S2, and the medial parietal cortices (155–56). Brain structures that provide "second order mapping," which makes the core self possible, are the superior colliculi, the entire region of the cingulate cortex, the thalamus, and some prefontal cortices (179–82). The autobiographical self is based on brain regions supporting neural patterns that are the substrate for images and for dispositions out of which images can be generated as recalled or reconstituted memories. These regions include early sensory cortices, higher-order cortices, limbic cortices, and some subcortical nuclei (219–22).

11. *Katha Upanishad*, in *The Ways of Religion: An Introduction to the Major Traditions*, ed. Roger Eastman, 3rd ed. (New York: Oxford University Press, 1999), 35.

12. Thich Nhat Hanh, *Living Buddha, Living Christ* (New York: Penguin Putnam, Riverhead Books, 1997), 16, 17. Another resource for assistance in accessing our sacred center is the "centering prayer" movement in Christianity. See Thomas Keating and Gustave Reininger, eds., *Centering Prayer in Daily Life and Ministry* (New York: Continuum, 1998). I thank Tom and Paula Fangman for calling my attention to centering prayer.

13. Hanh, *Living Buddha, Living Christ*, 14.

14. Ibid., 20.

14: In Harmony with Cruciform Nature

1. Noss and Noss, *A History of the World's Religions*, 9th ed. (New York: Macmillan, 1994), 391–95.

2. Thomas à Kempis, *The Imitation of Christ*, in *Readings in Christian Thought*, ed. Hugh Kerr (Nashville: Abingdon, 1966), 132–33.

3. Catherine L. Albanese, *America: Religions and Religion* (Belmont, Calif.: Wadsworth, 1981), 328.

4. Quoted in George C. Bedell, Leo Sandon Jr., and Charles Wellborn, *Religion in America*, 2nd ed. (New York: Macmillan, 1982), 315.

5. Huston Smith, "Tao Now: An Ecological Testament," in *Earth Might Be Fair: Reflections on Ethics, Religion, and Ecology*, ed. Ian Barbour (Englewood, Cliffs, N.J.: Prentice-Hall, 1972), 62–81.

6. Bup Jung, "Man and Nature," in *The Human Encounter with Nature: Destruction and Reconstruction*, ed. Christian Academy, vol. 5 of *The World Community in Post-Industrial Society* (Seoul: Wooseok, 1989), 92–99 passim.

7. George Williams, "Huxley's Evolution and Ethics in Sociobiological Perspective," *Zygon: Journal of Religion and Science* 23 (December 1988): 392–99.

8. Holmes Rolston, *Environmental Ethics: Duties to and Values in the Natural World* (Philadelphia: Temple University Press, 1988), 188–89, 192–232.

9. Ibid., 219.

10. Ibid., 269. In his recent major work, Rolston writes that "the Earth-system does prove to be pro-life; the story goes from zero to five million species in five billion years, passing through perhaps five billion species that have come and gone en route." Holmes Rolston, *Genes, Genesis, and God: Values and Their Origins in Natural and Human History* (Cambridge: Cambridge University Press, 1999), 364.

11. Rolston, *Environmental Ethics*, 225.

12. Holmes Rolston III, "Does Nature Need to Be Redeemed?" *Zygon: Journal of Religion and Science* 29 (June 1994): 205–29; Holmes Rolston III, *Science and Religion: A Critical Survey* (Philadelphia: Temple University Press, 1987), esp. 133–47, 286–93, 326–29.

13. John F. Haught also relates the Christian symbol of the cross to biological evolution: "In the symbol of the cross, Christian belief discovers a God who participates fully in the world's struggle and pain. The cruciform visage of nature reflected in Darwinian science invites us to depart, perhaps more decisively than ever before, from all notions of deity untouched by the world's suffering. Evolutionary biology not only allows theology to enlarge its sense of God's creativity by extending it over measureless eons of time; it also gives comparable magnitude to our sense of the divine participation in life's long and often tormented journey." John F. Haught, *God After Darwin: A Theology of Evolution* (Boulder, Colo.: Westview Press, 2000), 46.

14. Rolston, "Does Nature Need to Be Redeemed?," 211.

15. Ibid., 218.

15: From Life to Love

1. Carolyn McDade, "Spirit of Life," *Singing the Living Tradition* (Boston: Beacon Press, 1993), no. 123.

2. Mark 16:8.

16: Forsaken by God

1. Mark 15:34.

2. Acts 10:38.

3. Huston Smith, *The World's Religions* (San Francisco: HarperSanFrancisco, 1991), 328–29.

4. Bart D. Ehrman, *The New Testament: A Historical Introduction to the Early Christian Writings* (New York: Oxford University Press, 1997), 17 and 38.

5. My thinking here is based on a similar distinction by Henry Nelson Wieman, *The Source of Human Good* (Carbondale, Ill.: Southern Illinois University Press, 1946), 39–44. Wieman thinks that *love* is too problematic a term to talk about the divine as present in the relationships catalyzed by Jesus. He prefers to use terms associated directly with his God concept, namely transforming creativity. For him the cross and resurrection point to an event that releases this transforming creativity from the framework of first-century Judaism, represented by the man Jesus, "resurrecting" it to make it available for all people in "Christ the God."

6. 1 John 4:7–11.

17: At Home in the Universe

1. This Christian *understanding* was the same as that of the ancient Hebrews. See T. H. Gaster, "Cosmogony," in *The Interpreter's Dictionary of the Bible: An Illustrated Encyclopedia*, ed. George Arthur Buttrick (Nashville: Abingdon Press, 1982), 1: 702–9.

2. Quoted in Rudolf Bultmann, *Primitive Christianity* (New York: Meridian Books, 1960), 164–65.

3. Thomas à Kempis, *The Imitation of Christ*, in *Readings in Christian Thought*, ed. Hugh Kerr (Nashville: Abingdon, 1966), 132–33.

4. Eric J. Chaisson, "Cosmic Evolution: A Synthesis of Matter and Life," *Zygon: Journal of Religion and Science* 14 (March 1979): 39.

5. The metaphor of jazz first came to me when I read Arthur Peacocke's "Chance and the Life Game," *Zygon: Journal of Religion and Science* 14 (December 1979): 301–22, which is a slightly modified version of the third chapter of *Creation and the World of Science* (Oxford: Clarendon Press, 1979), 86–111. Peacocke develops the musical analogy with a Bach fugue. Following his lead, I thought that jazz also illustrated his point. Ann Pederson beautifully develops the jazz metaphor in her book *God, Creation, and All That Jazz: A Process of Composition and Improvisation* (St. Louis: Chalice Press, 2001). In her preface she credits a conversation with Peacocke as suggesting to her the "model of God as composer [and] also . . . that the improvisational arts of jazz and the blues might be the modern musical idiom for expanding a classical model of God and the world," p. vii. Peacocke himself comments on the significance of music in providing models for portraying God's creative interaction with the world in *Theology for a Scientific Age: Being and Becoming-Natural, Divine, and Human* (Minneapolis: Fortress, 1993), 173–77. He suggests that both the fugue and jazz introduce the idea of improvisation into "the model of God as composer [which] incorporates that element of open adaptability which any model of God's relation to a partly non-deterministic world should, however inadequately, represent," p. 175.

18: Earth: A Child of God

1. Charles H. Long, *Alpha: The Myths of Creation* (Chico, Calif.: Scholars Press, 1963), 35–145.

2. Sallie McFague, *Metaphorical Theology: Models of God in Religious Language* (Philadelphia: Fortress, 1982), 34.

3. Pierre Teilhard de Chardin, *The Phenomenon of Man* (New York: Harper Torchbooks, 1961), 180–83.

4. Rolston gives a nice summary of both lawfulness and inevitability on the one hand and contingency and probability on the other in *Genes, Genesis, and God: Values and Their Origins in Natural and Human History* (Cambridge: Cambridge University Press, 1999), 348–54.

5. Sallie McFague, *Models of God: Theology for an Ecological, Nuclear Age* (Philadelphia: Fortress, 1987), 59–87.

6. Gordon D. Kaufman, *God, Mystery, Diversity: Christian Theology in a Pluralistic World* (Minneapolis: Fortress Press, 1996), 101–9; *Theology for a Nuclear Age* (Philadelphia: Westminster Press, 1985), 30–46.

7. That a narrative could be a kind of argument was suggested to me by Karen Warren, "The Power and the Promise of Ecological Feminism," in *People, Penguins, and Plastic Trees: Basic Issues in Environmental Ethics*, ed. Christine Pierce and Donald VanDeVeer (Belmont, Calif.: Wadsworth: 1995), 217–19.

Suggestions
for Further Reading

In the last few decades the number of published works in various areas of science and religion has increased dramatically. My suggestions for further reading sketch only a few of the available resources. For those who wish to delve further into particular topics discussed in this book, the readings cited in the endnotes will provide some places to begin. In what follows I present some books that are related to the main themes developed in *Dancing with the Sacred*. Then I suggest additional resources for those who wish to read more widely in science and religion.

For those wishing to explore the nature of science and evolutionary theory, I recommend Ernst Mayr's *This Is Biology: The Science of the Living World* (Cambridge, Mass.: Harvard University Press, 1997). Mayr is one of the greatest biologists of the twentieth century. Now well into his nineties, he is still writing clear and insightful books that nonscientists as well as scientists can appreciate.

Another book about science is Ursula Goodenough's *The Sacred Depths of Nature* (New York: Oxford University Press, 1998). Goodenough, a cell biologist, describes clearly for the nonscientist some of the detailed explanations of biology. Calling herself a "nontheist" and a religious naturalist, she shows how science itself can evoke religious attitudes similar to those generated by traditional religious symbols expressed in poetry and music.

A Christian theologian who incorporates a scientific approach to religious thinking is Philip Hefner. In *The Human Factor: Evolution, Culture, and Religion* (Minneapolis: Augsburg Fortress, 1993) Hefner proposes hypotheses about how we might come to understand God's purposes and our own purposes for living in light of biological and cultural evolution. A key metaphor in Hefner's thinking is that human beings are related to God as "created co-creators."

For an evolutionary understanding of ourselves as human beings and what helps us find happiness and fulfillment, I recommend Mihaly Csikszentmihalyi's *The Evolving Self: A Psychology for the Third Millennium* (New York: Harper Collins, 1993). Writing in the framework of scientific naturalism that respects religion and offers religious insight, psychologist Csikszentmihalyi suggests that we have evolved to play a self-conscious role in the future evolution of ourselves and our planet.

Edward O. Wilson's latest book is *The Future of Life* (New York: Alfred A. Knopf, 2002). Another of the world's leading scientists, Wilson is a lover of all life based on what he knows as a scientist. In this book he says that the central problem of the twenty-first century is how to raise the standard of living of the poor while preserving the variety of other species as much as possible. He outlines how ethics, religion, science and technology, government, NGO's (non-governmental organizations), and private citizens can cooperate to address this problem and preserve the diversity of our natural world.

In my opinion, the best science and religion book of the 1980s is by Charles Birch and John B. Cobb Jr.: *The Liberation of Life: From Cell to Community* (Denton, Tex.: University of North Texas Press, 1988). Like Wilson, biologist Birch and process theologian Cobb combine a concern for the environment with social justice.

How we might find fulfillment in preserving our planet and diversity of life is the theme of Connie Barlow's *Green Space, Green Time: The Way of Science* (New York: Copernicus, Springer-Verlag, 1997). Barlow, a biologist, draws on science and on conversations with a variety of people in science and religion to present a readable account of how scientific knowledge can be united with a sense of the sacred, in order to provide meaning for our lives and guidance for living in harmony with nature.

Barlow is one of the scientists involved in the "creation spirituality" movement, founded by Matthew Fox and nurtured by Thomas Berry. A current leader of this movement is physicist Brian Swimme. One task of creation spirituality, and of many others in science and religion, is to develop a narrative of the evolutionary history of the universe that provides a sense of our place in the scheme of things and guidance for how we should live. This narrative is often called the "epic of evolution" or "epic of creation." Brian Swimme and Thomas Berry present this epic in *The Universe Story* (New York: Harper Collins, 1994).

Another presentation of the evolutionary epic and of reasons why it is so important today is Loyal Rue's *Everybody's Story: Wising Up to the Epic of Evolution* (Albany: State University Press of New York, 2000). Rue is a philosopher of religion who has steeped himself in science to the point that he can intelligently and accurately present science and show its significance for religious thinking today.

In *Dancing with the Sacred* I try to address environmental concerns with ideas from contemporary science and a variety of world religions. There are several theologians who are doing this. The one to whom my thinking is most closely related is Gordon Kaufman. In *God, Mystery, Diversity: A Christian Theology in a Pluralistic World* (Minneapolis: Fortress, 1996), Kaufman portrays God as ultimate mystery that manifests itself as "serendipitous creativity." He also views human beings as created out of biological and historical processes, and is concerned about how we humans need to take responsibility for what we are doing to our planet and to one another.

Another theologian who deals with environmental issues and religious pluralism is Jay McDaniel. While Kaufman and I develop nonpersonal understandings of the sacred, McDaniel uses a personal understanding of God, combined with aspects of Buddhism, to address the diminishment of the environment by a consumerist culture. I resonate with many of his ideas about spiritual living and enjoy the easy-to-read, personal style of *Living from the Center: Spirituality in an Age of Consumerism* (St. Louis: Chalice Press, 2000).

The central metaphor of my book is dancing with the sacred. At one point I also mention that the evolving universe is like jazz. Both metaphors present the dynamic, interactive nature of our world. The jazz metaphor is central in Ann Pederson's *God, Creation, and All That Jazz* (St. Louis: Chalice Press, 2001). Drawing on her own life experience, Christian theology, and modern science, Pederson suggests that our living is a process of composition and improvisation.

The problem of suffering is one of the important life issues addressed by religion, and much has been written about it from a variety of religious perspectives. An excellent summary and analysis of how religions address this problem is John Bowker, *Problems of Suffering in Religions of the World* (Cambridge: Cambridge University Press, 1999).

However, few people in science and religion explore very deeply the problem of suffering in an evolving world. In *Dancing with the Sacred* I draw on my own experience and the work of natural philosopher and environmental ethicist Holmes Rolston III. But much more needs to be done. One place to begin is with John F. Haught's *God After Darwin: A Theology of Evolution* (Boulder, Colo.: Westview Press, 2000). Haught is a Roman Catholic theologian, writing in the tradition of the Jesuit priest and paleontologist Teilhard de Chardin. His Christian evolutionary theology is suggestive for its comments on suffering, which are grounded in both science and religion.

Related to the problem of suffering is the problem of evil. In *Evil: A Historical and Theological Perspective* (Minneapolis: Fortress Press, 1995), Hans Schwarz provides a useful resource that surveys a wide variety of ideas regarding the nature of evil and its origins in behavioral science, psychology, the Bible, and Christian religious and philosophical thought.

In one of the few science and religion novels of which I am aware, Gretl Keren Fischer focuses exclusively on the problem of human evil and suffering in nature. *An Answer for Pierre* (Ottawa: Borealis Press, Ltd., 1999) combines elements from Judaism with a scientific view of the world to develop a naturalistic theology that responds to the enigmatic Pierre's question: "Why did God forsake the Jews in Auschwitz?" As she deals with this question, Fischer, a writer and a teacher of literature, creates an exciting personal and intellectual mystery.

The above suggestions will help the reader explore further some of the main themes in *Dancing with the Sacred*. For those who wish to read more widely in science and religion, here are some additional resources.

When I first began to study science and religion in 1966 at Columbia University and Union Theological Seminary, I was advised to read two things that had just appeared. The first was Ian Barbour's *Issues in Science and Religion* and the second was the scholarly journal *Zygon: Journal of Religion and Science*. That is still good advice. Barbour has a gift for digesting, classifying, and clearly presenting the rich variety of work that is going on in science and religion. One of his most recent books is *Religion and Science: Historical and Contemporary Issues* (San Francisco: HarperSanFrancisco, 1997). This book is often used as a textbook in college science and religion courses.

Three other comprehensive books, often used as texts, are by Arthur Peacocke, Holmes Rolston III, and Willem Drees. In *Theology for a Scientific Age: Being and Becoming — Natural, Divine, and Human* (Minneapolis: Fortress, 1993) Peacocke employs findings from a variety of sciences to develop a significant Christian theology. Rolston's *Genes, Genesis, and God: Values and Their Origins in Natural and Human History* (Cambridge: Cambridge University Press, 1999) is a careful, philosophical analysis of issues raised by contemporary biology for ethics and religious thought. In *Religion, Science, and Naturalism* (Cambridge: Cambridge University Press, 1996) Drees develops a naturalistic position as he considers the consequences of physics, biology, and the neurosciences for understanding how morality and religion are rooted in our evolutionary past.

Since 1966, *Zygon: Journal of Religion and Science*, edited by Philip Hefner and Karl E. Peters and published by the Joint Publication Board of Zygon (Malden, Mass.: Blackwell Publishers, 1966–), has been the major scholarly journal devoted to religion and science. It can be found in many college, university, and theological libraries. To see the variety of things the journal publishes, I suggest visiting the website of its publishing agent, Blackwell Publishers, at *www.blackwellpub.com*. Click on U.S. and, then, journals. Next type "Zygon" into the search box and click "submit." You will find authors, titles, and abstracts of articles published in the last five years.

Many of the books I have mentioned, as well as the articles in *Zygon*, have been stimulated and encouraged by the activities of a variety of science and religion organizations. These can be found by searching the Internet. When people ask me where to start the search process, I refer them to the website of the Institute on Religion in an Age of Science (IRAS), an organization that has been in existence since 1954 and of which I am a past president. Go to *www.iras.org* and click on "links" to begin discovering the many organizations in religion and science. These include the Center for Theology and the Natural Sciences, Berkeley, California, the European Society for the Study of Science and Theology, and the Zygon Center for Religion and Science.

Much work in science and religion is being supported by generous grants from the John Templeton Foundation. To learn about the Foundation and the kinds of activities it is interested in supporting, go to *www.templeton.org.*

One example of an enterprise supported by a Foundation grant is METANEXUS, the online journal directed by William Grassie at *www.metanexus.org,* 3624 Market Street, Suite 301, Philadelphia, PA 19104. With up-to-date notices of current activities in science and religion as well as articles and reviews, METANEXUS is a resource for people to survey and work with what is occurring in science and religion.

Finally, for those who would like a monthly newspaper, I recommend *Research News & Opportunities in Science and Theology* edited by Harold G. Koenig and Karl Gilberson, 415 Clarion Drive, Durham, NC 27705, and *www.researchnewsonline.org.* Short essays, book reviews, and news articles about science and religion make this publication attractive for both specialized scholars and the general public.

Index